NOVEMBER NOON

November Noon

Reflections for Life's Journey

Vivien Jennings, OP

Many blessings!
Sister Vivien

Paulist Press
New York / Mahwah, NJ

Library of Congress Cataloging-in-Publication Data

Jennings, Vivien, 1934–
    November noon : reflections for life's journey / Vivien Jennings, OP, PhD.
        pages cm
    Includes bibliographical references.
    ISBN 978-0-8091-4825-7 (alk. paper) — ISBN 978-1-58768-234-6
    1. Jennings, Vivien, 1934– 2. Dominican sisters—New Jersey—Caldwell—Biography. I. Title.
    BX4705.J455A3 2013
    271`.97202—dc23
    [B]

                                                        2012046100

ISBN: 978-0-8091-4825-7 (paperback)
ISBN: 978-1-58768-234-6 (e-book)

Published by Paulist Press
997 Macarthur Boulevard
Mahwah, New Jersey 07430

www.paulistpress.com

Printed and bound in the
United States of America

For Alice Jennings White—
Sister, mother, teacher, friend,
who, at age 93, is still showing us all
how growing old gracefully can be done in style

CONTENTS

CONTENTS

PART III—LIVING MORE DEEPLY / 87

PREFACE

Reading a book is making a commitment. "Do I really want to do this? Do I need this right now?" How many volumes have all of us started, thumbed through, and put aside? Hopefully, the volume at hand will offer a different experience. This is not a book on human psychology. We need something more than human solutions and self-help exercises, necessary as those may be from time to time. The pursuit of spirituality is more like hunger. "I'm hungry for something but I'm not sure what." So is it pride or folly that makes this author try yet again to capture an audience? Maybe it's both. Or maybe it's a need—a need to share the experience, to celebrate the journey.

Life IS the journey. WE are the journey. We who have lived life for awhile now need to reflect—reflect on all that's gone before, the joys, the mistakes, the "might have beens." Most of all, we need to reflect on what lies ahead—not to predict the future, just to live it more fully. If you share that felt need—the awareness that you're not yet where you're meant to be, that there's more in God's plan for you and that it's going to be wonderful—then perhaps this book is for you. If the format seems a little odd, I apologize. In each chapter, I draw significantly either from Sacred Scripture or from literature. We have such a well of wisdom in both the Hebrew and Christian Scriptures and we so rarely spend time to plumb the depths of their implications for our lives. Then there are the poets—yes, the ones we "had to read" in high school and college and never quite understood. Well, having lived life a little by now, I think I can guarantee that today we'll "get it," we'll really get it. I invite you to keep a notebook handy (dare I suggest a journal?) and jot down the "aha" moments as they come to you.

In the journey of life, place has a place. Everything that has happened to us has happened somewhere. We need to allow ourselves to revisit those places (perhaps journal about them), hear those voices, rejoice in those memories—or understand perhaps for the first time the pain we felt there. Because of the importance of place in each of our life journeys, I have introduced most chapters from a specific place through the eyes of a maybe-mythical character who, like us, is trying to advance on his or her life's journey. And so, remembered places, along with Scripture and poetry, will help to structure our passage through these pages (and through the pages of your journal should you choose to keep one).

Finally, a word about the title, *November Noon*. November can be a blah month. All we see around us is a dull terrain and uneventful gray weather. In the world of nature, November doesn't seem to be a very productive month. The land lies fallow, except perhaps for the winter wheat fields of Minnesota. No spring flowers or colorful autumn leaves decorate the hills, and the winter snow has not yet come to paint the lawns. November just *is*—a little like us in our later years, feeling a bit colorless, no longer needed perhaps, less useful to the world around us—or even like those in time of transition or temporary underemployment, stepping back from some position of importance or influence. Yes, everyone has his or her November. When that time comes, we need to refocus and adjust to the new "season."

And there's also *Noon* in the title. Half the day is already spent but half (or some) still lies ahead. We feel a touch of urgency because we know we can still get something done, let someone know he or she is loved, deepen our relationship with God—all those things we thought we'd do "someday."

I hope that reading these pages may help us refocus and see the landscape ahead more clearly, much more lovingly. *Carpe diem*. Let's begin the journey together.

I

LIVING FAITHFULLY

And Jesus said: "Ask, and it will be given you; search, and you will find; knock, and the door will be opened for you." *Luke 11:9*

I

SEASONS OF OUR LIVES

The wind howled as it wrapped around the big old house. Windows rattled and a loosened shingle clattered on the rooftop. With effort Miss Annie rose from the frayed rocker and made her way to the window. "First snow," she mused. "No walk outdoors tomorrow." Every season brought its own challenges now that the arthritis had taken such hold. But gently she recalled the childhood memories in this very place. How her heart had danced at the sight of snowflakes because it always meant building that first snowman on the lawn as soon as Daddy came home from work.

For some of us, the image of Miss Annie is like looking in the mirror. The limited mobility that comes with aging, the inevitable confinement, the occasional hours of quiet loneliness...and yet, like Miss Annie, we can let the good memories suggest a positive response. An hour later, when the doorbell rang, she was prepared. Bobby, the neighbor's boy, leaned heavily on his shovel. "Finished your walkway, Miss Annie," he reported. "I salted it, too. Should be safe to walk on in the morning." Annie wanted to give him a couple of dollars for the favor but she knew his mom would only send him back with it, Instead, she said, "Now that sure was kind of you, Bobby. I made a little apple pie this afternoon. I'll bet you could finish off a piece right now." Like any hungry teenage boy, he couldn't resist. Off came the boots and he was at the table before she could ask again.

As it happened, Annie had more to offer than pie and milk that day. "You look a little worn out today," she said. "Was the snow really frozen?" "It wasn't that," Bobby admitted. "It's just that, well, I got a little bad news in the mail. You know, Miss Annie, I'm not much of a student even though I really try. I applied to State for college admission and their letter came today. I'm not exactly rejected, but they suggested I defer till next semester. My dad's gonna be really disappointed."

Well, there it was. It's a painfully competitive world out there and it starts very early. Young people, too, experience rejection and disappointment in dreams and, with it, a loss of self-esteem. Happily, Annie realized that this was the real reason she was meant to encounter Bobby today. "Well, Bobby, there's more than one way to skin a cat," she said philosophically. Thirty minutes later he had completed his application for the local community college with wise guidance from Annie, a former teacher, as to what courses would best prepare him for the transfer to State after one or two semesters.

The fact is that every season is made up of so many sunsets, whether we see them or not. If we can just let ourselves be the instrument of bringing the warmth of a little sunshine into someone's life each day, that's the day we'll see a sunset. If it happens every day, we've made a week of sunshine. And the weeks are just the building blocks of a very good season.

The seasons of the year punctuate our lives. We are forever filled with expectations. When will the leaves begin to turn? When will we see the first snowfall? When will the first crocuses emerge? *Turn, turn, turn.*...Yes, the rapid rush of the seasons reminds us of the dance of nature, which invites us each year to take part in the dynamic cycle of life.

Like the world of nature, human life, too, has its seasons. Youth's vibrant springtime finds its fulfillment in the achievement of adulthood when one finally feels "in charge." Then a mellow maturity lends perspective to all that has gone before until, at last, life's winter strips us of the unimportant, only to

4

reveal the true beauty of inner strength—the "instress of the inscape" as Gerard Manley Hopkins called it.[1]

Of course, we recognize the comparison but some of us have yet to grasp the rest of nature's lesson, namely, how best to prepare ourselves for the change of seasons. In the natural world, even amidst the lushness of summer, beavers are busily gathering wood for their winter dams. And, as autumn peaks, squirrels have gathered their nuts for the lean months ahead. In winter we observe hibernation among some creatures, but also the steady application of survival instincts—gathering, storing, pacing of energies—until the first bursts of a new springtime.

The seasons are often seen as a metaphor for the phases of human life. Spring, summer, autumn, and winter can be considered as paralleling youth, early adulthood, maturity, and old age. But a deeper spiritual insight allows us to realize that the experience of *every* age can include—indeed, must include—many a spring day. Dawn comes, the sun rises, and a new day is here. The feeling of youthfulness is identified with the new light of day. Henry David Thoreau wrote: "Only that day dawns to which we are awake. There is more day to dawn. The sun is but the morning star."[2] One is never too old to meet the dawn. This is an important truth that younger relatives and caregivers would do well to remember. Each time we choose a dawn—try something new, change up an old recipe, try a new mode of prayer, read an unfamiliar Scripture passage—we pursue a dawn and the day is young again.

Sometimes, dawn struggles to emerge. The long dark night hangs on, and sickness, worry, disappointment can delay dawn's coming. Like a courteous guest, sometimes it waits to be invited. Lightness of step, a cheerful demeanor, humming a tune (even mentally) are all signs that dawn has come. We should cultivate that youthful time of day every day. It will water the seed of a lightsome spirit, which becomes the rich soil to receive God's grace. God uses our natural human disposition to shape our spiritual lives. Thus, pursuing the dawn at any age is not only a pious desire; it's also good mental health.

5

JOURNALING

What new dawn do you anticipate? How much do you believe in it? How joyfully do you prepare? What is your favorite season? Why? What memories from your younger years do you associate with a happy season? What is the longest season for you? Why is that? Was there a painful loss that occurred in that season? A lost relationship? Can you take steps to heal the memory?

2

FRAMEWORK OF FAITH

Victor was the night security guard on campus. A well-spoken Englishman, he had retired to America when his only son married a lovely lass from Rhode Island. Although he lived in an off-campus apartment, Victor usually took a late dinner in the student dining hall before going on duty. That's how I got to know him. I had the same pattern once a week before teaching an evening class, and I frequently chose to eat at Victor's table, away from the noise of the students. Our conversations often took a philosophical turn. One night he seemed more pensive than usual. Finally, he asked: "Dr. Johnson, do you believe in God?" "Why, yes, I do," I replied. "Well, I never have," he confessed. "I guess it was just never part of our upbringing....But last night as I walked the campus and looked up at that magnificent winter sky all flecked with stars and the moon shining bright—I tell you, I wondered...." It's been years since that night but I sometimes wonder if Victor ever said his "Yes" to faith.

Those of us who grew up in a Christian household surrounded by believers came to understand at a young age the traditions and practices of the faith. We never realized the strength we drew from the faith-filled community that surrounded us, both family members and neighbors who often attended the same church and lived their lives by the same norms. Decades later, for some that framework of faith may have become just a distant memory or, even more sadly, a source of bitterness and regret. But there are also some, like Victor, who may simply never have been exposed to any faith.

As we grow older, our worlds widen. No longer are we surrounded by tight-knit neighborhoods filled with people who share the same faith or even the same values. Diversity in school and workplace, along with the pace of life that leaves little room for personal reflection, can also contribute to a false homogenizing of our values. Rejection of authority and a desire to assert one's independence are also factors, especially among the young. For those of us who now find ourselves living outside the framework of faith, it may be hard to remember what led us to this point. Often enough, people don't make a conscious decision to reject faith. It may just be a matter of drift—an occasional omission that grows into a comfortable habit. After a while we find "reasons" to justify our situation. The bad example of a dedicated churchgoer, the scandal of pedophilia, a newspaper article about the mishandling of church funds—these are certainly sad examples of human weakness but they needn't be allowed to weaken our faith.

In the four or five decades since many of us were young, the world and the Church have changed dramatically. Many practices have changed, but our core beliefs have not. Saint Paul tells us: "And now faith, hope, and love abide, these three; and the greatest of these is love" (1 Cor 13:13). These are known as the three theological virtues, directing and strengthening each person's relationship with God. They are well named because the word *virtue* comes from the Latin word *virtus*, meaning "strength." We tend to think of a virtue as some good habit that we "practice" as if on our own, but in fact it's God's gift to us to keep us strong as we pursue the spiritual journey.

This is the real framework of faith, an anchor we can cling to in the turbulent sea of a confusing time. As we begin to unwrap this framework, we realize that nothing happens by accident in the plan of God. We have undertaken to read this book at this moment in time. Hopefully, these pages may guide us

8

toward the deeper waters of the spiritual life, surely God's plan for each of us. Or they may provide a way back, ideas that may help us to correct our course if we've gone adrift. And who of us has not? At the very least, they may offer a more contemporary understanding of our once-vibrant religious values.

As we set out on this spiritual journey toward a more intense awareness of God in our lives, faith is our starting point—faith in an unchanging, all-powerful, and loving God. What else do we believe? We believe in Jesus Christ as our personal Savior, in the certainty of God's all-forgiving love, in the promise of eternal life. And even after being adrift in the sea of life's challenges, we do still believe in these things—intuitively cling to them like a life preserver in choppy waters. This kind of faith is pure gift. We cannot "acquire" it by simply willing it. Nor can we increase it of our own volition. That is God's domain.

Why does one person have the gift of faith and another does not? Only God knows. It is possible for someone to "discover" faith. Sometimes people search their whole lifetime for "that larger truth" and finally arrive at an intellectual assent. But even then, only the gift of God's grace allows them finally to embrace faith. Such was the case with John Henry Newman, whose humble prayer during his time of searching was the now-famous "Lead, Kindly Light." He wrote: "Lead, Kindly Light, amid the encircling gloom.... / The night is dark and I am far from home.... / I do not ask to see the distant scene.... / Lead Thou me on."[1] The light of faith guided his spiritual journey. Newman was beatified in 2010.

Hope, too, is a theological virtue. As such, it is so much more than empty optimism. Spiritual hope disposes us to expect God's gifts, to understand that God wants the best for us. God says, through the prophet Jeremiah: "I know the plans I have for you... plans for your welfare, not for harm, plans to give you a future full of hope" (Jer 29:11). Why then do we waste so much time in worry? Ninety-nine percent of our worries never come to pass.

Isaiah, too, has a hopeful message: "When the poor and needy seek water, / and there is none.... / I, the LORD, will answer them.... / I will open rivers on the bare heights, / and fountains in the midst of the valleys" (Isa 41:17–18). We who are committed to working for justice or to providing community service can become that "river on the bare heights" for someone in need. Every day we encounter people suffering in the desert of poverty, oppression, or personal need. By our caring action we have the power to offer them hope.

It's important to understand that hope is not just about tomorrow. Let us remember the promise: "I, the LORD your God, / hold your right hand" (Isa 41:13). Not past tense. Not future tense. God holds my hand...right now! We need to allow ourselves to feel God's presence—in this moment, in this place, not just in imagination. God is real in our everyday lives. But if our hands are so full of material things, or so full of the tools of the everyday, or so full of worries about tomorrow, even God can't grasp that right hand. How many such moments have we missed already?

"What does the LORD require of you / but to do justice, and to love kindness, / and to walk humbly with your God?" (Mic 6:8). I have come to love this quote from the prophet Micah. It seems to me to offer a spiritual synthesis, an all-embracing rule of life. Only lately have I come to see it as paralleling the three virtues of faith, hope, and charity. "Walking humbly with our God" is the simple expression of our faith. Surely, only a believer can do that. And "to love with kindness" identifies the theological virtue of charity. But where is hope in Micah's synthesis? "Acting justly" is the very embodiment of hope. For who can act justly without hope? We hope that our actions will make a difference, hope that God will multiply our efficacy to extend our actions to all in need, hope that systems will finally change so as to embrace systemically God's plan for the human condition.

Consider once again Saint Paul's reminder of the primacy of love in the hierarchy of God's gifts. The experience of human love prepares us to understand the gift, which is Divine Love. Even human love is so much more than a feeling. At its bedrock level, it is an exchange of commitment, a pledge of wills, and an engagement of hearts that is reciprocal and lasting. Human love in this understanding seeks to reflect the paradigm that is Divine

Love, which, knowingly or not, all humans long for and which God longs to bestow. Actually, the two kinds of love—human and divine—are intertwined. The First Epistle of Saint John reminds us that we cannot say we love God and yet hate our neighbor. Writing from the perspective of personal friendship with Jesus and his own advanced age, John says, quite simply, "Beloved, let us love one another, because love is from God" (1 John 4:7).

The important learning here is the primacy of love as the identifying characteristic of the Christian. At the end of our journey, we will not be asked how many rosaries we've said or how many awards we've won. We will be asked nothing less than how much we've loved—loved God, loved others, loved life, which is, after all, God's gift to us. "Love is patient; love is kind" (1 Cor 13:4), Saint Paul admonishes us. All of us know and have experienced the generous love of friends and neighbors who unselfishly extend a helping hand in time of need, who go well beyond the call of duty in helping others. Surely we ourselves have done the same.

Now here's the challenging question: Do we do as much for God? Does God have any claim on our time each day? As we begin once again to take seriously the invitation to live a deeper spiritual life, we need to recognize the importance of this question. At its core, love is about fostering a relationship, and that takes time. It takes being present to the other, to the Other. So building in that time for quiet reflection on God's word in Scripture and for reverent openness to God's initiatives in our daily lives is essential. These, above all, will be the moments that water the seed of spiritual growth, of greater intimacy with the God who first loved us.

JOURNALING

Reflect on the patterns of your days over the past week. Note whether loving time was spent in presence to others, and thank God for that grace. How much time was given to thoughts of God? How attentive were we to God's thoughts of us, to the subtle presence of God's grace? Write down a schedule for spending daily time in this presence and try to be faithful to it.

3

THE CALL TO HOLINESS

I climbed quietly up the sloping lawn to the point and stood for a long time looking down the embankment to the rushing river below. Flowing down from its source in the Falls, the waters moved mightily, two hundred feet below the retreat house grounds. Just above the riverbed stretched the tracks of the New York Central Railroad. Now more than a hundred years old, the ancient landmark is more than a sentinel to a bygone era. Every morning and evening, the Metro North trains rumble north and south along the riverbank, carrying commuters to and from New York City. On this warm autumn afternoon, that great metropolis seemed far away indeed. Finally, I sat down, journal in hand. I tried to come here every few months, at least once in each beautiful season. This spot was my favorite reflection site here at the retreat center. Many an afternoon I took an imaginary journey through the wooded Palisades that rise majestically just across the water. Today, I was filled with gratitude.

Gratitude is the perfect starting point—and gazing on the beauty of nature, an ideal setting—for the time of prayer. Such a setting disposes us to begin with a simple prayer of praise for all of Creation and for the goodness of our all-loving Creator God. But a time of retreat three or four times a year? Impossible! Maybe so, depending upon one's present responsibilities and one's state in life. But a short dialogue three or four times a day? Quite manageable, actually. This is an invitation from a personal God who loves us deeply. It is not simply a decision on the part of the one who prays. And while a ten-day retreat at a nearby monastery might seem like a wild luxury, how about a precious ten minutes apart with God several times a day?

Despite all the goodwill in the world, how does anyone manage such time? Immersed as we are in the demands of everyday life, it requires a deepening focus and a certain daily discipline. Controlling the noise that surrounds us might be a good start. Could we begin by not turning on the radio in the car as we do the daily errands? Consciously choosing to give up one or two hours of television viewing might also free our attentions for reflecting on more spiritual realities. When not in the contemplative setting of the bank of the Hudson River described above, I choose to go there in my imagination. Call to mind any such contemplative scene and rest there with the Lord. Talk to him gently, then listen, too. Prayer, after all, is a conversation. Yes, it may well take the whole ten minutes just to quiet down. That's all right. The whole rest of the day will be different just because of this tiny effort to converse with God.

This will all seem like an effort at first—an effort to forget the argument we just had with our neighbor, or to stop worrying about the doctor visit later today. Try to turn it all over to God in the first few minutes of the prayer time, and then, temporarily at least, to let it go. After all, God knows all our needs before we name them.

When it's time to return for the second prayer period of the day, this may be a challenge. We need to have a plan and, if possible, a space. After lunch, if weather permits, step outside the house or office. If nothing else, a breath of fresh air will do us good. Take in the scope of nature, and it will feed our spirit for hours. Back at the computer? Quietly lift up our minds and hearts to God before turning our attention to the technology. Mentally offer a conversational acknowledgment of the Lord's presence before picking up the phone or returning to the ever-present household chores. Reverently and silently recite the Hail

13

Mary or another familiar prayer. "Short on time today, Lord, but I know you're still with me. Show me what I can do better this afternoon. Let your peace prevail in my life throughout the rest of this day. Let me be your presence in the lives around me." Simple, loving thoughts will flow. Be yourself.

No matter if we're still in the workforce, already retired, or recovering from an illness, it may seem that we should have more control over our prayer time, but that isn't always the case. Creating a prayer schedule takes discipline. Keeping to some simple schedule is important—not for God but for us. The human condition is such that we need to prove to ourselves that this is important—in fact, a priority. If you have young people in the family, it probably drives you crazy seeing them texting all day long, weekends included! And if they're courting or engaged, the communications seem to be nonstop. "Those stupid machines! They ought to be banned!" But it's not about the technology; it's about being in love. Surprise! These two people have to find a way to let each other know they're thinking about each other, can't wait to see each other. That's also the meaning of prayer time throughout our own day—thinking about God, reminding God that we want to be in his presence, that we need to hear his voice. (God, of course, is not the one who needs the reminder!)

Finding the third prayer period of the day may be a little easier. Again, maybe not for the working mom or dad, who not only may have to help the children with homework and get them to bed, but in addition may be taking an online course that's usually not even gotten to until 10 p.m. Well, no one said this prayer thing would be easy! But ten minutes? "I can do this." As the house quiets down, find the perfect space. Maybe it's a comfortable chair in the living room. If there's a tranquil painting on the wall, all the better. Enter into that scene—the summer garden, the scenic snowfall, whatever. Put yourself there, then quietly, humbly, look back at the day. Allow yourself to feel God's presence. Without getting bogged down in the details, thank him for all of it, above all for his loving care—for just being there even when you weren't thinking of him, for carrying you when the need came, for giving you courage when you didn't think you had it on your own, for protecting your loved ones when you couldn't be there to do it yourself. That's real prayer. Again, gratitude.

Developing and keeping a modest prayer schedule without rigidity is essential if one is serious about deepening one's interior life. But why should we even care to do that? So many really good Christians keep the Commandments, go to church regularly, live wholesome lives, and strive to bring up their families to live according to Christian values. They're fulfilling the obligations of being good Christians, but often they don't experience the quiet consolations that come from intimacy with their God. The busy flow of daily life seems to consume them before a personal relationship with the Lord can be fostered. As with so much in life, wishing will not make it so. I remember as a teenager attending a friend's piano recital. She played magnificently. I turned to my mother, who had accompanied me, and said, "I wish I could play like that." And you can imagine her response: "When was the last time you practiced?" Relationships, like talents, need to be developed, practiced. The daily prayer times may seem like practice sessions at first. We start with a lot of goodwill, get interrupted or discouraged, and have to start again. But that's okay. Isn't that the familiar pattern of love—starting again?

Hopefully, we all know someone whom we regard as really "holy." A pious grandmother, perhaps, or an elderly pastor. They seem to radiate peace, project a steady equanimity. Their charity seems effortless. Once in a while we may even say to ourselves, "I wish I could be like that." With great wisdom, the bishops at the Second Vatican Council responded to this reality. In the now-famous document *Lumen Gentium* (the Dogmatic Constitution on the Church), the bishops declared: "The Lord Jesus... preached holiness of life to each and every one of His disciples, regardless of their situation: 'You, therefore, are to be perfect even as your Heavenly Father is perfect....Thus it is evident to all people that all the faithful are called to the fullness of the Christian life and to the perfection of charity."[1] (ALL the faithful, not just priests and sisters and the pious elderly.) And again: "All are called to sanctity and have received an equal privilege of faith through the justice of God."[2] This inspiring section of the Vatican II document has come to be known as "the universal call to holiness." So, as we begin to pursue a deeper relationship with God, let us consider ourselves truly "called." God invites us; he awaits our response.

Talking about prayer is hard. The act of praying requires effort, and yet it is all gift. Clearly, ten minutes, three times a day, is only a beginning. We will be moved to prolong the time, look for better occasions, prepare some basis for the prayer experience. Surely, there are many times in life, and even in a short span of life, when we find it necessary to change: change careers, change technologies, change our attitudes. All of us need to dispose ourselves toward beginning again, many times over. This is as true in a person's prayer life as it is in one's professional or family life. Let's remember that, each time, change has the potential to be exciting, even life-giving.

One thing we may want to change in relation to our prayer is how we prepare for our time with God. Scripture can be an excellent springboard to prayer. Many possibilities exist here. Select one of the four Gospel accounts—Matthew, Mark, Luke, or John—and read it through reflectively from beginning to end over a period of a month or so. Taking the time to do that is not prayer time itself but preparation for prayer. Then, in the daily prayer time, return to a short passage that has touched you as powerful, meaningful, even just familiar. Read a few lines slowly and reflectively, praying for insight into the meaning of this passage and for a deeper understanding of God in your life. In the monastic tradition, this practice of prayerful reflection upon Sacred Scripture was known as *lectio divina*, "sacred reading."[3] As you become aware that the reading has turned to prayer, cease reading and let God speak directly to your heart. If distractions arise, return to the text and continue reading the passage at hand. After the prayer period has ended, try to return to the content of your prayer several times throughout the day. If the actual subject of your prayer can't be remembered, that's all right. You will at least recall God's presence and be reminded to praise him again!

JOURNALING

Have you attempted to move into a slightly longer prayer period based upon scriptural reflection? Write down briefly your experience. Did it seem like real prayer with an awareness of God's presence? Or was it more like reading a page of history, a bit academic? What new awareness do you take from this time apart? What might you do differently to prepare a more prayerful focus?

4

PRAYING WITH SCRIPTURE

The teenager set aside her workbasket and looked toward the half-door that revealed the setting sun. Time for afternoon prayer. She so looked forward to this time of day, when all the household chores were done and it was still too soon to prepare the evening meal. This was *her* time. She rose and moved toward the half-open door. Across the fields, lengthening shadows played with the fading sunshine. Spontaneously she prayed her favorite psalm: "The heavens are telling the glory of God; the firmament proclaims his handiwork. / Day to day pours forth speech, and night to night declares knowledge. / There is no speech, nor are there words, yet their voice goes out through all the earth" (Ps 19:1–4). Suddenly there was a rustling sound behind her. She turned and gasped at the unfamiliar image.

"Greetings, favored one! The Lord is with you.... Do not be afraid, Mary....You will conceive in your womb and bear a son, and you will name him Jesus" (Luke 1:28–31).

But Mary *was* afraid and very puzzled. How could this be? Like all pious Jewish women, she had been praying for the coming of the Messiah but never did she think....Finally, she found her voice: "Here I am, the servant of the Lord; let it be with me according to your word" (Luke 1:38).

Mary spoke her "yes"—and what a yes it was, reverberating down through the centuries! She was accustomed to spending quiet time with her God, a time on that day that left her "available" to the angel's invitation. She was not afraid to raise questions but her "yes" was prompt and generous, trusting her future to God's plan. Would we have been that trusting? Would our hearts even be still enough to hear the invitation? In order to pray this scriptural moment more fully, place yourself in the room with the young Mary. Are you sitting or standing? At what angle to Mary? To the angel? What is it that you first see? A hint of fear on Mary's face? A single tear on her young cheek? Listening intently, what do you hear? The rustling arrival of the angel? His hopeful, heavenly words? Mary's prudent objection? Her ultimate, whispered yes? Bring your reflection into the present. Be aware of what invitation, what challenge of grace, God is offering to you today. Saying your "yes" will change your life, as it did Mary's.

The fact is that we will probably not be visited by angels. Nevertheless, God's invitation comes in many forms every day. An elderly relative needs some groceries. The next-door neighbor needs a ride. A grandson's class needs a chaperone, or their field trip will have to be canceled. How many times a day do we say a generous "yes" without even recognizing that this is an invitation to do good, to touch lives, to make a difference? We need to take some time at the end of each day to reflect on the invitations to service that we received. Did we use each as an opportunity to make a difference by our cheerful, caring attitude? Or were we just doing the next task with little or no reflection?

The Annunciation passage in Luke is just one example of using Scripture to feed our prayer life. Many people find it satisfying to use a daily missal, which contains the scriptural readings for each day's liturgy. When this is fruitful for your deeper reflection, by all means use it. But when those specific readings seem not to speak to you because the sequence of your life's experience is not necessarily the same as that of the liturgical cycle, you need to find an alternative. Go back to reading one of the Gospels—Matthew, Mark, Luke, or John. Refer to your journal if you are keeping one, and find a scriptural passage or two that spoke to you in the past. Often it will be a familiar passage that stayed with you because you could identify with that event in the life of Christ or because you could see yourself as one of the participants in the scene. Find the passage again, reread it, and perhaps use that for several days as the basis for your prayer. Remember that we read Scripture this way, not as an academic exercise, but in order to come closer to Christ, to become more like him, to become a part of his salvific plan for the world.

Take, for example, the Epiphany, that early moment when Christianity went global! The arrival of the Three Kings from the East instantly widened awareness of Jesus' mission to all peoples. His "rule" was not to be limited to the local community of Bethlehem. It is interesting that Matthew's is the only one of the four Gospels to include the visit of the Magi. These men had done their homework. They had traveled for a purpose and they asked questions. "Where is the child who has been born king of the Jews? For we observed his star at its rising, and have come to pay him homage" (Matt 2:2). They may not have understood his divinity but they were certain of his royalty. Hence, the gifts they brought included gold (the appropriate royal gift), as well as frankincense (used in formal ceremony such as prayer), and myrrh (an exotic eastern product sometimes understood as a foreshadowing of Christ's suffering).

As we enter personally into this unique scene, where do we find ourselves? Perhaps in the background with the shepherds, who have stepped aside so that the kings can approach. Or perhaps near Joseph, who stands protectively behind Mary and the Child, still not quite understanding all that's taking place. As people of faith, we bring our own greeting to the Christ Child before pondering the meaning of all that is before us. These visitors in strange garb serve to remind us of the larger scope of Christ's mission. They make us wonder how far *we* might be willing to go to find the Redeemer. There are moments in our lives when God seems far away indeed. Do we ever bring gifts to Jesus when we meet? Is there some special gift that only you can bring, not to Christ for he needs no gift, but to his world today? And notice the inclusiveness of Jesus, Mary, and Joseph, welcoming strangers from a distant land.

In our parishes today, the color and language of our congregations are changing dramatically. How does that make you feel? Have you chosen to greet or visit with any parishioner who may be from a different culture? Have you encouraged one of your own grandchildren to invite that neighbor's child for a playdate? These are simple forms of inclusivity that must be the hallmark of today's truly catholic (meaning "universal") Church. And we ARE the Church. Christ told his followers: "Go therefore and make disciples of all nations, baptizing them in the name of the Father and of the Son and of the Holy Spirit" (Matt 28:19–20). That mandate is meant to begin at home.

Then there is the story of the Woman at the Well (John 4:7–42). Jesus, ever the teacher, reminds the apostles that a moment of ministry can await us when we least expect it. Jesus "just happened" to be passing through Samaria on his way to Galilee. Likewise, a woman "just happened" to come to the well for water. Jesus initiates the conversation as a good minister often does. "Give me a drink" (John 4:7). He uses this as a stepping-stone to get the woman to reveal herself. When he asks for her husband, she admits she has no husband, and Jesus reveals his awareness that she has had five husbands. His intimate awareness of her sinfulness does not stand in the way of his continued conversation. Had he stopped there, the moment of salvation would have passed. Instead, he seized the moment and revealed himself as the Messiah. When the woman hastened into town to tell her neighbors, they came to see and hear for themselves. "It is no longer because of what you said that we believe, for we have heard for ourselves, and we know that this is truly the Savior of the world" (John 4:42). This Bible story has become a favorite of women's spirituality groups for obvious reasons. As we pray with this text, we need to ask ourselves: For what do I thirst? With what disposition do I receive God's gift of "living water"? Do I allow myself to reveal honestly God's gifts so that others may be brought to him?

These Gospel reflections can be taken as just three examples of the rich sources for prayer that daily Scripture reading can provide. The method of placing ourselves into the scriptural setting is suggested by the Ignatian approach to the "prayer of the imagination."[1] That phrase is a good reminder that all of our human faculties have a role to play in our salvation journey.

JOURNALING

Refocus on one of the three scriptural passages discussed above and reflectively answer the questions posed for that passage or others that suggest themselves to you. Conclude with a sincere resolution to take a practical step to deepen your awareness of God's presence in your daily life.

5

EXPLORING THE PSALMS

Traveling through Vermont on an autumn vacation, Helen and Don decided to visit the monks at Weston Priory. They had written ahead and made reservations to stay at the Guest House for a night. "I thought we were on vacation," Don groaned as the clock went off at 5:30 a.m. Always encouraging, Helen pleaded, "But it will be so beautiful to hear the monks chanting the psalms of the Divine Office to welcome the new day!" "Yeah, and with my luck, it will probably be in Latin," Don grumbled.

For the Christian seeking to deepen his or her spiritual life, the psalms can be a worthy vehicle for proclaiming God's praise, even when our human nature lacks the words or energy to express our own devotion. There is a rich body of scholarship around the psalms, and many competent analyses of individual psalms are available. As with other topics presented in this volume, this is not the place to go into a deep academic analysis of this sacred topic. Several worthwhile sources are available,[1] but some basic information can be offered here by way of introduction.

The psalms are the poetic centerpiece of the Hebrew Scripture. They express the joy, laments, praise, and contrition of the Hebrew people as they lived through their period of salvation history. Expressed in the voice of the Psalmist, they reveal the drama of God's interaction with all his people and of their human response. Still central to Hebrew prayer today, the psalms also provide the language of praise for Christians as well.

23

As our friends Don and Helen (above) discovered at Weston Priory, the monks and cloistered nuns throughout the Christian era have kept the use and the study of the psalms alive down to the present time. They form the core of what is known as the Liturgy of the Hours, which Catholic priests are obliged to say in its entirety each day. Also known as the Divine Office, the Liturgy of the Hours is meant to punctuate the day, making the entire day an offering of praise to God. In the monastic tradition, Morning Praise is preceded by an Office of Readings, usually in the early hours of the morning. Additionally, Midday Prayer is offered at the noon hour. Evening Prayer, or Vespers, is followed by Compline, which is considered the Night Prayer of the Church.

As an aid in the deepening of our prayer life, we may want to consider the practice of praying a few of the psalms twice each day. I suggest twice a day because, as explained above, that practice will unite us with the praying Church as the psalms of the Divine Office are being prayed in all the religious houses throughout the world, as well as by pious laity who have joined in this practice. Some parishes, especially those led by priests of religious orders, have begun praying the Office in the parish church or chapel. If such exists in a nearby parish, I suggest that you attend occasionally as a way of deepening your own prayer life. On a recent visit to Paris, I had the privilege of praying Vespers with the congregation at the famed Notre Dame Basilica. Despite the unfamiliar language, tourists from all over the world were united in their devotion and profoundly aware of their union with the Church Universal. I couldn't help thinking what a powerful effect this could have on world peace if only this experience could become more widespread!

In beginning the practice of praying the psalms, it may be helpful to be selective. Because of their varied subject matter—with warlike images or references too tied to Hebrew history to be understandable—some of the psalms don't lend themselves to personal devotion. So I offer here an introductory look at just three psalms that may be said to be more "user friendly." Included in the notes are ten additional psalms that may also prove to be comfortable aids to prayer.[2] Note that the psalms are usually referred to by number, indicating the order of their appearance in the Book of Psalms within the Hebrew Scripture. In addition to the psalm number, they are also often identified by the first line, which frequently expresses the theme of the psalm.

We should acknowledge at the outset that people with busy work schedules and family obligations may find it difficult to add psalm prayer to their period of scriptural meditation on a daily basis. Devotional practices can't substitute for two good prayer periods that include Scripture reading and quiet reflection. This is where one is likely to meet his or her personal God in prayer, without using someone else's words. But if psalm prayer is occasionally undertaken, one may begin to see a unity in all of it. The psalms, which have a unique prayer value of their own, also feed one's reflective time so that one's spiritual life becomes quite seamless.

We begin with Psalm 19, a beautiful prayer of praise extolling God's glory as Creator. The Psalmist begins: "The heavens are telling the glory of God; / and the firmament proclaims his handiwork" (Ps 19:1). The statement is universal and unequivocal. Unlike many contemporary poems, there is no doubt about the intended meaning. "There is no speech, nor are there words; / their voice is not heard; / yet their voice goes out through all the earth" (v 3–4). The magnificent imagery captivates our imagination. "[God] has set a tent there for the sun; / it comes forth like a bridegroom from his chamber, / and like a strong man runs his course with joy" (v 4–5). The sun as a bridegroom and as an athlete running his course is imagery that evokes a powerful response from anyone who has ever contemplated the natural beauty of sunrise and sunset. It gives new meaning to the greatness of all creation. The only response is the prayer of gratitude to the Creator of such majesty.

This is what prayer is made of. One can read the psalm over and over again and suddenly the "wow" moment comes upon us. The second part of the psalm compares the law of God to the majesty of nature's beauty. The repetitive rhythm of each short phrase adds to the poetic experience. Often the psalms were sung or accompanied by a harp or zither, which helped to focus the musical experience. The Psalmist continues: "The law of the LORD is perfect, / reviving the soul; / the decrees of the LORD are sure, / making wise the simple" (v 7). The movement of the final section is personal. In light of the greatness of creation, God can certainly forgive my sins. "Clear me from hidden faults.... / Do not let them have dominion over me.... / Let the words of my mouth...be acceptable to you" (v 12–14). The movement of the poem—from praise of creation, to recognition of God's law, to personal contrition and supplication—makes for one unified and flowing prayer. As with the reading of any poem, each repeated reading reveals new meaning and new beauty.

Let us look next at Psalm 27, expressing and praying for trust in God. "The LORD is my light and my salvation; / whom shall I fear?... / Though an army encamp against me, / my heart shall not fear" (Ps 27:1, 3). It would be easy to skip past the phrasing of verse 3 with a dismissive "This doesn't pertain to me." But if we understand the reference to *army* as any strong adversity, even temptation, the line takes on real meaning. In the following verses the language mellows. "One thing I asked of the LORD, / that will I seek after: / to live in the house of the LORD / all the days of my life" (v 4). This is one of my very favorite lines in all of Scripture. The more you engage with the psalms, the more you will discover your own personal gems, lines that speak to your heart and feed your prayer. The tone of tenderness and trust continues: "Even if my father and mother forsake me, / the LORD will take me up" (v 10). Indeed! And the final line brings us back to the awareness that life is a struggle: "Wait for the LORD; / be strong, and let your heart take courage; / wait for the LORD" (v 14). This psalm, too, offers almost a whole compendium of the spiritual experience. As with all good poetry, universality is key.

Finally, Psalm 34 offers an extended prayer of thanksgiving and instruction on fear of the Lord. Fear of the Lord, as we remember, is one of the gifts of the Holy Spirit, but once we learned that in our Confirmation classes, we probably haven't thought much about it since. *Fear* is not a popular word, and some contemporary writers tend to omit it from their vocabulary for "fear" of alienating timid readers. But we've all experienced fear, either of physical danger or a health risk, or other such threatening moments. Still, *fear* is not a word we like to associate with an all-loving God. But fear of the Lord, like the other gifts of the Spirit, is intended to strengthen the Christian in virtue. We can best understand it in the context of fearing to displease God as we would fear to displease a loving parent, not out of dread of punishment but out of an unwillingness to disappoint his or her expectations of us.

That said, let's look more closely at the words of this beautiful psalm. "I will bless the LORD at all times; / his praise shall be continually in my mouth. / My soul makes its boast in the LORD; / let the humble hear and be glad. / O magnify the LORD with me, / and let us exalt his name together" (Ps 34:1–3). In this short opening stanza, the Psalmist exclaims his praise of God and explains his reason "that the humble may hear and be glad." Then, as now, the poor don't always have many reasons to be glad. And finally, the invitation to his audience to join him: "Magnify the LORD with me; let us exalt his name together." Do we ever dare to invite others to join us in the act of prayer? Do we consciously invite the poor to join in our parish prayer groups? Do we even notice that they're missing?

In part three, the Psalmist offers a "teaching," a short, instructional discourse on human behavior. He encourages his listeners to avoid evil and not to speak lies. (Note that we speak of listeners, not readers, since there were no readers in the Psalmist's day. The Book of Psalms was part of the great oral tradition.) "Seek peace and pursue it" (v 14). The whole of the virtuous life is summarized in that one saying. And the final consolation: "When the righteous cry for help, the LORD hears, / and rescues them from their troubles. / The LORD is near to the brokenhearted, / and saves the crushed in spirit" (v 18–19). In the sometimes powerful events that punctuate human life, as we enter into intercessory prayer either for ourselves or those we love, remembering those lines alone can be a saving grace.

If we prayed just these three psalms daily for a week until they became somewhat familiar to us, we would be developing a base of comfort on which we could expand this prayer experience. Then, beyond just reading and understanding the psalms, we could move toward really praying them. And it helps to remember that each time we pray the psalms, we are united with the praying Church throughout the world in a paean of ongoing praise to our God. As we do so, the inadequacies, distractions, and preoccupations that we may experience are compensated for by the holy attention of others at prayer. A consoling realization!

JOURNALING

Select one of the three psalms discussed above, or one of your own choosing. Read it slowly as you reflect on its meaning. Then read it again as a poem, not one line at a time, but honoring the punctuation by reading to the period. (These are sentences, after all, even though often printed in indented lines.) Finally, read it once more as a prayer, your prayer. Write down your experience of this third reading. Try to do this with one psalm each day, noting your experience in your journal. A word of caution: There are various versions of "contemporary psalms" available today. While some offer more familiar vocabulary, they may not offer the depth of biblical meaning. Working with the Book of Psalms included in an approved edition of the Bible that offers an authentic translation may prove more valuable to you as a basis for prayer.

6

WITHIN A FAITH COMMUNITY

The academy was located on a sprawling, twenty-acre campus. Beautifully maintained, the lawns laid out a cordial welcome in every season. But dressed in winter white, they were just gorgeous. Sister Kristen was, by necessity, a frugal administrator. So when she announced that ten young pine trees had been purchased for planting around the main building, everyone was surprised. In the days after the planting, it was evident that she had found "a bargain." Scrawny twisted twigs stood bravely against the snow. Poor Sister Kristen took a lot of teasing. When asked why they were planted so far apart, she answered, "They'll need the space to stretch their branches when they grow." Her hopeful words were met with laughter, even by the students.

It's now been fifty years since the trees were planted. Recently, when I visited the campus for a fifty-year class reunion, I stood in amazement before the tree-lined vista. Eight hardy pines stretched almost to the fourth floor of the building! (Yes, two of the original plantings hadn't made it.) I had to think that Sister Kristen believed in her trees just the way she believed in us: "Leave room for the growth."

It seems to be part of the human condition to be impatient with our own faults and failings, and heaven knows, they are many!

This can be a source of great discouragement as we try to move forward in the spiritual life. At the same time, because we are trying so hard to be better people, we become even more sensitive to our own lack of tolerance with the shortcomings of others. In both cases, Sister Kristen's advice may be helpful: "Leave room for growth."

Human behavior is just that: it's human. Our actions are the product of our human dispositions, emanating from personality traits that have been long in the making. As the psychologists tell us, we are the products of both "nature and nurture"—that is, what and who we are naturally, as well as how we have been "nurtured" by influences that surround us (family and society). This combination makes us human, and the lifelong challenge is to become the best human person we can be. Even in the purely human order, most people work very hard to maximize the good traits of their personality and to minimize or eradicate their darker tendencies. For the person of faith, this is not merely a human effort, nor is it accomplished by free will alone. When we spoke of the virtues, we acknowledged that we can't acquire them just by willing it. But, relying on God's grace, we strive to grow in the life of virtue, not just for our own perfectibility, but in order to share in the building of the kingdom.

We say, when praying the Our Father, "Thy kingdom come." What does that mean? Do I mean just that I will get into the kingdom of heaven? On the contrary, we are praying for the coming of God's reign ("kingdom") here on earth, beginning in the present moment. How does this happen? An honest child would say, "Too slowly!" The well-motivated Christian shares that impatience. If the coming of the kingdom doesn't mean just within ourselves, what then? "No one goes to heaven alone" has become a commonplace among Christian preachers. We are social beings, meant to belong, meant to enter into relationships with others. In the Vatican II document *Decree on the Apostolate of the Laity*, we read: "The laity have an active part to play in the life and activity of the Church."[1] The document continues by quoting Christ, who said:

30

"Where two or three are gathered together for my sake, there I am in the midst of them" (Mt. 18:20).

For this reason the laity should exercise their apostolate by way of united effort. Let them be apostles both in their family communities and in their parishes...as well as in voluntary groups which they decide to join.[2]

Whether we ever saw that quotation before or not, since the Church began implementing the outcomes of the Vatican Council in the late 1960s, we have certainly experienced that philosophy in action in the renewed structure of our parishes. Pastoral councils, parochial school boards, Scripture study groups, and social justice committees are only a few of the now-common groupings that call for our service and participation. These are all examples of the Church's efforts to "open the windows" to the modern world and to mobilize the collective wisdom and energies of each parish congregation. Yes, I said "wisdom." Thanks to the Holy Spirit, we all have some piece of wisdom to be shared for the bringing about of the kingdom here on earth. As we attempt to shift our focus from the possibly frenetic pursuit of busyness to a more prayer-centered way of living, we can't forget the value—indeed, the blessing—of moving forward with other prayerful Christians.

Psychologists point out that the human tendency to socialization is profoundly meaningful, and that our engagement with ever-widening circles of community signifies maturity. Such professional commentary only confirms our own experience. We recognize that we can accomplish more together than we can as individuals, whether our efforts are in behalf of social outreach, improved liturgy, or any other goal. Idealistic? Perhaps. Those of us who have spent the last four decades (or more!) trying to translate that idealism into reality may be feeling a little weary just about now. So we take it to prayer and ask ourselves: What would Jesus do? He'd likely go up to the mountain to pray to the Father. Then he'd probably have tried to get some sleep before the crowds of the new day came to him. And then he'd keep on speaking the Father's word. Admittedly, it's hard to measure results. But these are important needs and we have only the present moment. So we stay at it together and try to make it all work.

Occasionally, at least, we need to look at the makeup of all the small communities we're part of. How is each of our "circles" different from the others? Is one "wider" just because it's a larger grouping? Look at the diversity. Does everyone in this group or on that committee look just like us? Is there any representation from other races, other cultures? It's so easy to say, "Well, none of them live in our parish." THEM? Our very answer exposes the problem! Every one of our groups needs to be enriched by the diversity of perspective and experience that can be brought by people of color, by those of other cultures and socioeconomic backgrounds. Otherwise, the various committees and prayer groups we're part of can become just the same folks wearing different labels, and the richness of ideas is lost.

In addition to having diverse backgrounds, every group is made up of widely varying personalities and temperaments. An interesting activity for groups to engage in is to take the Myers-Briggs assessment[3] or some similarly objective measure of personality traits. Interpretation of the group results by a trained counselor can be quite enlightening.

Whatever the makeup of our groups may be, as individuals we need to examine our personal priorities from time to time, as well as the quality of our personal involvement. The first circle of importance is our family. At different ages we hold different levels of responsibility to spouse, children, parents, and siblings. As some family members grow more independent, others grow more dependent, and circumstances of geographic distance and even death bring changes in our relationships. Because our focus here is on being human, we want to look at our relationship with our family members especially as it pertains to our Christianity and our own spiritual life. If we are of an age where we have direct responsibilities for family members, even our desire for wider involvement in social outreach or more religious activity should not supersede those responsibilities. Keep in mind that doesn't include the necessity of attending every Little League game or class play! For the parent whose job won't suffer or the teenage sibling who has flexibility in his or her day's activity, this may be a worthy show of support to the young family member. However, for the grandparent or great-grandparent, it's not essential and need not be a source of anxiety (or even anger) if you find yourself without a ride to the game and another family member doesn't have time to provide one.

Some may recall when, as younger parents, you were often pulled in two directions—between needful children and aging parents. You're called "the sandwich generation." And now, as lifespans lengthen, you might still be in this situation even as a grandparent yourself. Once again, balance is key, isn't it? And that's easier said than done. That is when the evening reflection on your day might have been so very helpful in the past. Even now, reviewing briefly (without reliving) the demands of the day just passed and how you handled them can be immensely beneficial. Consider not just what you did but how your spirit was affected. If your response in some instance was not consistent with your desire to live the Gospel through your interactions with others, what might you have done (or said) differently?

This kind of exercise can raise our awareness of our own humanity and of the spiritual dimension of the day's interactions. It can and should also provide a framework for our participation in all of our "circles." The social justice committee we're on and the Scripture-sharing group we're in are both made up of human beings with the same human weaknesses and strengths that we have. Therefore, it should not surprise us that someone in the group occasionally offends us or that the group as a whole gets involved in criticism that devolves into uncharitable conversation. It's important to evaluate our participation in that and be prepared to speak the unpopular word if necessary to bring the group back to its Christian, Gospel-centered purpose.

Of course, our levels of interaction are not limited to those suggested above. If we're now living less active lives—for example, in an assisted living or a nursing home environment—we may tend not to see our companions as persons in one of these "circles." But the neighbors who sit at our dinner table or with whom we may watch TV are those we encounter every day.

Examine once in a while how we interact with these folks as well. Does our Christianity show consistently in our kindness, forgiveness, and cheerfulness among them? Many of these companions may not have our background. Yet their needs are the same—just hoping to be treated in a kindly manner, hoping people will be patient with them, hoping they'll see a cheerful smile. Our Gospel reflections on our daily behaviors may help to soften our own dispositions and in turn allow the light of the Gospel to shine through. The historian Tertullian recorded what he saw as the hallmark of the early Christian communities: "Behold how they love one another!"[4] What a privilege it would be to be so identified!

JOURNALING

Reflect on Jesus' warning against judgmentalism among his disciples (Luke 7:37–42). Or reflect quietly on the implication of the quote from Tertullian above. Then select just one hour out of the last twenty-four and see how your interactions in that hour compare to the Christian ideal. Did you remember Sister Kristen's admonition to "leave room for growth"? Make some realistic resolve for tomorrow.

7

COMING HOME

Jim and Phil met at the coffee shop as they did most mornings. "So, what'd you do, oversleep this morning?" Jim asked. Phil looked puzzled but before he could ask, Jim explained. "So, where are your ashes, man? Today's Ash Wednesday. You *are* Catholic, aren't you?" "Forgot all about it," Phil answered, somewhat chagrined. "Anyway, I'm not so much into church stuff these days." "Sorry, Phil. None of my business. I was just wanting to tease you. With all the Irishmen in this neighborhood, the ashes are almost part of the uniform today."

Later that morning Phil saw Jim walking his dog, so he stopped to apologize. "I hope I wasn't abrupt with you before, pal. You know I'm divorced, remarried ten years ago. So I guess I'm just outside the pale for now." "No, I'm the one who should apologize. I didn't mean to pry. But as long as you're choosing to talk about it, do you mind if I ask: Have you ever inquired about this? Talked to a priest at your parish?" Phil answered honestly, "The pastor at our church looks like my baby brother. I don't think he'd understand. Besides, it's been a while...."

How many of us have found ourselves in a similar conversation? Maybe the setting was different but we've been there—either receiving the information or trying to explain it. Such moments are providential: a casual inquiry, and the respondent is almost

35

glad to be asked so he can talk about it. In our efforts at courtesy, let's not miss that moment. What a graced time if we have the chance to extend understanding or, more importantly, to provide accurate information or suggest the name of a wise pastor who can help the person sort things out. Above all, we should avoid being judgmental and respond with compassion and humility. Who of us is perfect?

Currently, 22 million people in the United States identify themselves as "former Catholics." According to a recent study by the Pew Forum on Religion and Public Life,[1] one in three persons who were raised Catholic has left the Church. Of these, many have joined various Protestant denominations. One half are "unaffiliated." Until recently, less attention has been given to this decline because it has been largely offset by the influx of immigrants who are enrolling in our parishes across the country. Nevertheless, the withdrawal of some 22 million baptized Catholics calls out for closer analysis.

Myriad reasons underlie this reality. Some people report that they have become disenchanted with the Church's teachings. Often, this observation pertains to the Church's social teachings, such as its stance on the death penalty, the antiwar statements of the American bishops, and so on. For some ultraconservative individuals, the Church seems too liberal, and for the ultraliberals, the Church will never be liberal enough. Where the disagreement is with moral teachings or theological doctrine, it touches closer to home because it affects personal behaviors. In trying to assist a disaffected Catholic in one of these areas, we simply have to acknowledge that the faith we embrace is not a matter of "pick and choose." Our responsibilities in some areas are nonnegotiable. It's not always easy, but as people of faith, we believe that the grace will be there to strengthen our resolve.

Although the Pew Forum research cited above focused on Catholics, this phenomenon of departing from one's original church affiliation is not unique to the Catholic Church. Other mainstream denominations report a similar occurrence. Some who have separated themselves from their original faith community report that their spiritual needs were not being met. They name poor liturgies, poor preaching, lack of pastoral concern, unwelcoming environments, and generally "uninspired" parish life as major concerns. These are the same issues for many who remain in active membership. While we work to change some of these circumstances, especially through our own active participation as liturgical leaders and members of parish life committees, we need to remember that the Sunday liturgy is not the totality of our faith experience. Our spiritual lives, just as our physical lives, are meant to be lived fully every day. That is where some of the pages of this book may be helpful in strengthening our daily religious experience through more active reading of Scripture and a regular discipline of personal prayer times.

We also know that we will not always succeed in fulfilling our obligations. Within the Catholic tradition, the sacrament of Reconciliation is there both to help us face our shortcomings and to seek God's mercy. But for those who have been separated from the Church for some time or for what they perceive to be serious cause, the sacrament itself may seem like a stumbling block. There may be several reasons for this. The memory of being scolded in Confession as a child, a certain fear or timidity that impedes communication, an inadequate understanding of current teachings, or inaccurate information from others—any or all of these become reasons for not approaching the sacrament of Reconciliation when it's needed most. Perhaps the best approach is to initiate a conversation with one of the priests in a local parish and then sit down in conversation with him at an unhurried moment. Often, such a dialogue becomes the sacramental moment that one has been hoping for, sometimes for years. Many psychologists assert that Catholics are fortunate to have the sacrament of Reconciliation, which offers an opportunity to experience support and guidance and to unburden oneself from a sense of guilt instead of suppressing it for years on end. Even if these circumstances don't pertain to us, perhaps they offer some thoughts that might be shared with another in need when the opportunity presents itself.

Whatever the original cause, the longer we're away, the harder it is to return. We say in the Apostles' Creed: "I believe in the forgiveness of sins, the resurrection of the body, and life everlasting."[2] If we really believe that, then we must give up being our own judge. Only God can say if a person has been away "too long," and that doesn't sound like something God would say. Reflecting on several relevant Gospel scenes will remind us of practical examples of God's infinite mercy.

First, recall the parable of the Prodigal Son. He took his share of the inheritance and squandered it all. Then, after many a trial, he was moved to return home. "How many of my father's hired workers have more than enough food to eat, but here I am dying of hunger. I shall get up and go to my father" (Luke 15:17–18). Not the most perfect motivation, was it? But the loving father didn't even question his son's return. He just rejoiced, as any loving father would. In fact, he threw a party to welcome him home! Jesus told that story to remind us of God's loving mercy, no matter what. It's not hard to place that family example into a contemporary setting. How often a broken relationship requires the intervention of a loving mother, who convinces her angry husband to put aside his pride and pick up the phone, no matter how long it may have been or who was originally to blame. We all have that loving mother in Mary. Not without reason is she known as Our Lady of Mercy and Friend of Sinners. As Pope Paul VI once wrote: "We believe that the Holy Mother of God, the new Eve, Mother of the Church, continues in heaven to exercise her maternal role on behalf of the members of Christ."[3] We need to seek Mary's intercession often both for ourselves and for others.

Another relevant example from Scripture is the cure of the paralytic (Mark 2:5–12). Remember when Jesus was preaching and the crowd was so great that the friends of the paralyzed man actually made a hole in the roof and lowered the man on his mat into Jesus' presence? (That's what friends do—they bring us into God's presence!) When Jesus saw the man, the first thing he said was: "Your sins are forgiven" (v 5). Then, because he was aware of the thoughts of the Pharisees, he said to them:

"That you [the Pharisees] may know that the Son of Man has the authority on earth to forgive sins"—he said to the paralytic— "I say to you, stand up, take your mat and go to your home." (Mark 2:10–11)

Most of us know from experience that when we ask God to heal us, the healing is never just physical. This is a powerful thought to remember when we pray for a cure! We may not be prepared for the completeness of God's response.

And finally, when Jesus was on the cross, the man who has come to be known as "the Good Thief" rebuked his companion who was mocking Jesus and then said: "Jesus, remember me when you come into your kingdom." And without hesitation Jesus said: "Truly I tell you, today you will be with me in Paradise" (Luke 23:42–43).

The examples from Scripture could be multiplied. The point is the universality of God's mercy, as revealed in the redemptive mission of Jesus. Whether it is meant for us ourselves or for someone we care about, the message is clear: It's never too late to "come home."

JOURNALING

Revisit, slowly, one of the Scripture passages cited above that reveals God's consistent mercy. In your journal, write a brief reaction to the passage. Can you cite any recent example of your own forgiveness of someone? Of your own deep desire for forgiveness, either from God or from a loved one?

II

LIVING PROPHETICALLY

What does the LORD require of you
but to do justice, and to love kindness,
and to walk humbly with your God? *Micah 6:8*

8

RESETTING THE CLOCK

Still pretty vibrant at the age of seventy-three, Bill had finally decided to retire. "This'll make room for one of you younger guys," he joked. His wife, Daisy, had retired several years before. She was delighted at Bill's decision, yet, knowing him so well, she had her reservations.

As we pause at the threshold of our later years, fatigue may lead us to shout: "I've changed enough already!" Indeed, that's true. Major sociological and technological changes have taken place in the last fifty years. Global warfare...social, ethnic, and seismic shifts...computers and iPhones...a communications revolution that has shrunk our world—remembering it all can leave us breathless. But we've survived. Not only that, for the most part, we have thrived. So we trust our instincts, we trust our God, and we can move forward.

Still, these years of older maturity may require more adjustment than the average person expects. The last child is off to college or recently married. A needy relative may have gone now to the Lord. We've cut back from a full-time job to half-time, or perhaps we're now fully retired. Whatever the particular circumstances, we're likely to find ourselves with a little more flexible, if not entirely free, time. This may be the Lord's gift, his way of offering a bit of leisure to read a longer passage of Scripture, pick up a new spiritual book, say a rosary for world peace, or get out to a noonday prayer service or Mass at the local church.

The recently retired may have even more of an adjustment. After a few weeks of well-deserved rest, they begin to find questions arising. People like our friend Bill, above, start to ask: "What do I do with myself now?...Maybe this wasn't a good idea...This was a really long day...I'm not used to not being needed."

Then come the financial doubts. We read and reread the numbers sheet that we prepared (hopefully with some advice) in the months leading up to our decision. Now the reality of the first month of bills begins to set in, along with the first (and maybe the only) monthly check reflecting the fixed income. "I just hope this is really going to work. Maybe the cable TV will have to go." Yes, if we're of a certain age, we've been through it all in one scenario or another. Whether we're alone or with a spouse, these times can be very emotional. While staying on top of the practicalities to the extent possible, the answers to the other questions may lie in a simple decision to reset the clock: the body clock, of course, but also the inner clock, that "drive to do" that is so characteristic of modern living. "But how many novels can I read? How much day-time television is even worth watching?" Clearly, that's not such satisfying activity for one who's been accustomed to deadlines, decision making, and responsibility.

Resetting the clock begins with embracing this new moment of life. It's not about taking up new hobbies, joining a bridge club, or buying more gardening tools (all worthy activities, to be sure!). Resetting the clock isn't about filling up the day. For the person of faith, it's about finding our way with God's help into a new terrain. That extra time for prayer, for regular periods of reading Scripture, for keeping a spiritual journal that really leads us somewhere—this is the time to prove to ourselves just how serious we were when we used to say, "How I wish I had time for all that!"

But how do these retirement issues relate to "living prophetically"? Reflecting on this new condition of life can move us toward understanding the invitation to live more justly and toward finally having the time to do it! As our days become less structured, we may find opportunities to observe the neighborhood or church community to see who's in need, who's alone, who's in the nursing home waiting for a visitor. We may begin to feel called to a volunteer ministry. If so, test this in prayer: "Am I really being called by the Lord—or just by my need to keep busy?" Then weigh the obligations against whatever other responsibilities we already have. Who at home has a claim on our time? Can we do this new service prayerfully? We can test it by writing in our journal: Is this just a diary item about the day, or did it have spiritual meaning for me and for the other person? These questions reflect a person who understands the difference between ministry and just another task. They can help us to recognize what a gift it is to live each new day at a more leisurely pace, stopping to "smell the flowers" or to just call a friend.

JOURNALING

Read reflectively the Scripture passage of the miraculous catch of fish (Luke 5:1–11). Jesus takes humble fishermen who make their living from the sea and in an instant makes them "fishers of men," that is, disciples who will feed human souls because God is empowering them to do it. In a single moment their "work" is transformed into "mission." Have you experienced God's power working in your own life in a similar way? In your journal, record the experience and its meaning in your life.

LIVING THROUGH CHALLENGE, LONELINESS, AND LOSS

Richard was an accounting major, heading with enthusiasm into his senior year. He planned to sit for the CPA exam before moving on to NYU for the MBA program. That summer he began to experience some vision problems so he decided to see a specialist before returning to campus. After the routine office exam, the doctor ordered a few X-rays. The tests revealed a growing mass on the ophthalmic nerve. Richard was stunned, knowing that his whole future was now shrouded in uncertainty. Because he had such trust in his doctor, Richard moved forward with surgery, which was successful in removing the tumor. After a semester away from the books, he was able to return to school and pursue a bright future.

We've all known alarming moments—times when things were not certain, times when we knew the future was not in our hands. We can't predict how we'll respond in the future, but it may be helpful to recall moments in the past when profound challenges have faced us. Perhaps, like Richard, we've experienced a serious health situation that threatened the future, or perhaps a financial reversal that caused us to lose independence. Whatever the crisis, how did we react? Emotional responses are natural at such times. In fact, they're healthy and should not be entirely stifled. But we need to be able to go deeper than that. Can we, even now, turn those circumstances over to God, try to discern a life-giving response so as not to yield to despair? However hard and unnatural it may seem, we need to try to move forward in trust with joyful fortitude. No one can do this alone. We need to acknowledge our helplessness (a hard thing for twenty-first century Americans) and ask for God's grace.

These reversals are not "God's doing" and we may err in referring to them as God's will. God never reverses our free will, and many of the negatives we experience are the result of our own free choice. We choose to smoke, and we get lung cancer. We consistently choose rich diets, and then we develop diabetes or heart disease or any of the dangers that come with obesity.

Financial reversal may be more circumstantial. We become victims of a worldwide economic downturn or we lose our job because the company is downsizing. Such things are not "our" fault but neither are they God's fault. Therefore, we cannot let them weaken our faith, take away our hope, or dampen our love. The answer lies in trust, that special grace that allows us to "hang on," knowing that God is still in charge.

You may be thinking that, while these things are true, they hardly belong among thoughts about living prophetically. Anyone experienced in the spiritual life will tell you that if we do not address such practical issues, they can be a persistent obstacle to prayer. The prophets spoke loudly about the injustices of their day, but they knew personal suffering and even persecution as well. We have only to think of Job and Jeremiah to be reminded of that. Their compassion for the needy of their world was deepened by the personal suffering that they themselves endured.

The world today is in the grip of suffering. Perhaps that's been true for centuries. But anyone living in this second decade of the third millennium will certainly agree that it's true now. The devastating losses of 9/11 and its aftermath; the U.S. military engagements in Iraq and Afghanistan; the tsunami in Indonesia; the devastation from Hurricane Katrina; the oil spill in the Gulf of Mexico; Japan's earthquake, tsunami, and nuclear disaster—the litany of events has left a global trail of grief. In addition to these, there are political, social, and economic realities. The world's economy has experienced turmoil. In the United

States alone, banks and billion-dollar corporations have had to be "rescued" by government bail-outs. Unemployment has been higher than at any other time since the Great Depression. Returning veterans, whether they bear grave injuries or not, will not even talk about the horrors of war that they've seen.

Just writing this list is simply heartbreaking. Yet for so many of us, after the first week of television coverage, these tragedies become remote. Suffering becomes personal when it's *my* son's brain tumor, *my* husband's heart attack and sudden death, *my* incurable macular degeneration. These are the moments when we turn to God and scream in anger—as if he's caused it. And it's all right. God can take it. God knows that, for many of us, that's the first expression of prayer. The anger is not really at God but at our own powerlessness to change the situation, to make things better for those we love. In the past, we may have read articles on the subject of human suffering and the need for trust, but until we're in its grasp, it's merely academic. Patient endurance is a nice phrase until we're the ones who need it!

Though we may not see the connection right away, the habit of praying with Scripture—especially in preparation for, and celebration of, the major religious feasts—can be a profound help in a time of crisis. Take, for example, the story of Richard that opened this chapter. In addition to being a bright young man with a promising future, Richard was a devout Jew. With his pious family, he had observed the Passover with its readings and rituals every year since childhood. At the moment of his first grave diagnosis, Richard realized that this was his crisis moment. He knew he was supported by the prayer of his family and friends and that helped him to trust. When the successful surgery was over and healing began, he knew that this had been his Passover. Finally, he understood what the great feast was all about. And every year after that, he celebrated in a whole new way.

For many of us, suffering is not a comfortable subject, and when we're confronted with it, we often lapse into platitudes. "Why did God let this happen?" Or, "It must be God's will." Are we talking about the same God? God promised us, through the prophet Jeremiah, "I know the plans I have for you,...plans for your welfare, not for harm" (Jer 29:11). God doesn't cause human suffering. He wants our happiness. We have only to look at the life of Jesus in Scripture to realize that. During his years on this earth, Christ never inflicted harm on anyone, not even his enemies. And neither does God do it now. Our God is a God of compassion, that is, he "suffers with" us as we endure human tragedies. His presence to us is what makes it possible to endure, to trust, and to survive. We need to develop a new personal theology of suffering that is rooted in a prayerful and frequent reading of the New Testament that introduces us on every page to the God who loves.

Most of us have already lived through many losses in our lifetime. The death of a loved one, that ultimate earthly separation—the memory of it never leaves us. Nor would we want it to, because remembrance is a form of *re*-membering, of being with that loved one in another way. If you grew up with the custom of visiting the family gravesite, you know that feeling. You're not just visiting the gravesite but the memories, the times together, the joys and sorrows shared. We welcome such moments even though they may bring tears. These are the times that foster compassion, that free us to be present to others with truer empathy.

I remember, for example, hearing about little Jocelyn, who was just four years old when her father died—killed in the collapse of the World Trade Center where he worked. Jocelyn's young world was shattered. Now a teenager, she doesn't have a clear memory of that day. But she knows she has a hole in her heart that is very real. Even though I don't know her personally, because of my own experience of loss, I can empathize with Jocelyn and pray for some healing to come to her. Compassion is a tender gift—the capacity literally to "suffer with" another. If we ourselves never knew loss, we wouldn't understand another's pain.

But there are other losses, too: loss of a friend through some misunderstanding, loss of a job that brings fear for the future, loss of physical capacity through illness or aging, and the impatience with self and others that inevitably follows—such are the darker threads of the human experience. As such, they have the power to humanize us if we dare to name them.

49

Such losses, even loss of health or physical capacity, are usually events, moments in time that can be named. Loneliness often flows from such events, but it helps to understand that loneliness itself can be a separate issue. Loneliness is the experience of missing another or others, a sense of absence that carries with it unique and sometimes lasting feelings. We may think of it as a negative thing but in actuality it can be a sign of a healthy personality. To feel bad that someone is missing is to acknowledge our affection for him or her when they were present. When we can name for ourselves that we used to feel good when that person was around—relative, friend, spouse, or neighbor—we are admitting to our normal feelings of past love or affection. This can serve as assurance that we're capable of those feelings in the future if we can just get through this "patch of the lonely desert" as I like to call it. No one would choose to remain in the desert. Even John the Baptist and Jesus after forty days of "testing" chose to return to their active mission in due time. So must we.

I almost named this chapter "Living *with* Challenge, Loneliness, and Loss," but the word *with* suggested no end, just endurance. The one who wants a healthy, balanced life finds the path back to it by passing *through* the current challenge. It doesn't mean we'll ever forget the loved one whom we miss. It simply acknowledges that the loved one would want us to be our normal, caring selves again, and would want others to know us as they did—the cheerful, kindly, wholehearted person who had so loved them and continues even now to love life. Yes, tears will still flow and that's healthy—but hopefully, as we remember our dear ones, we'll remember the good times, too, and the laughter we had. Then the smiles will break through the tears and we can face the new moment. In fact, in some strange way, we face it together.

We are, after all, people of the resurrection. If we truly believe that Jesus Christ rose from the dead, we cannot doubt that his desire for our good can bring us through even the most difficult of human loss. Yet, in spite of our faith in the Risen Christ, loneliness may persist. There are times when a loved one's absence from our lives is almost as tangible as his or her presence. We know that feelings of loneliness can be healthy. But holding on to those feelings, choosing to isolate ourselves for too long a period, is not healthy. It can lead to disengagement and even to depression, which is far more serious than loneliness. Trying to repress these feelings of loss or sadness in order to appear "okay" only pushes them deeper down inside of us, until we deny even to ourselves that they exist. If you happen to be in my senior age group—or if you're of the same ethnic heritage (a detail I leave for you to guess!)—you may be more inclined to repress negative feelings. You may have been exposed to such phrases as "Big girls don't cry." Well, guess what—they do! And that's okay. What's not okay is to repress the sadness and to act as though nothing's ever wrong. If that becomes a pattern, it can lead to depression, which may require medical or psychological intervention.

Periods of grieving may be caused by many things—the death of a loved one, moving to a new location, an unwelcome retirement, increasing physical disabilities, a serious falling-out with a longtime friend. After a brief period of realistic coping, it becomes important to monitor our daily behavior. At the end of a long day of feeling "down," whatever the cause, resolve to face the next day more brightly. Make a plan to punctuate the new day with two or three simple strategies: for example, after lunch (regular meals are very important!), sit on the porch and greet a passerby; take a short walk or drive to a nearby store just to get some human interaction; or even call a friend. Then when you awake the next day, DO the things you planned. You may even find that the friend you call needed to hear from you even more than you needed to talk. Meanwhile, try not to neglect whatever prayer routines you've built up. Return to these, not out of obligation, but because you know you need the interaction with God even more than with your friends.

Hopefully, this daily effort—and it will be an effort—will enable you to feel more "normal." As we return to a moderately cheerful pattern of life, we gradually become more like ourselves. Isolation is never healthy. This is all part of living *through* the loss rather than *with* it. Whether large or small, these human sufferings of ours take on redemptive value when we pause to unite them—and ourselves—to the sufferings of Jesus Christ. In the Gospel narrative (Matt 27:46), we hear Jesus on the cross cry out in the familiar words of the Psalmist: "My God, my God! Why have you forsaken me?" (Ps 22:2). Yes, even Christ, the God-man, experienced a sense of abandonment that he might show us the way of perseverance in love.

As mentioned above, one factor that can cause a powerful sense of loss is the awareness that we may be losing our independence. This is often related to increasing physical limitations due to advancing age or diminished health. I have a friend who can never visit a nursing home because she sees her own future in the face of every patient. Unlike some of the kinds of loss we've discussed, the loss of independence is not usually related to an event. Rather, it is the experience of a gradual sense of diminishment related to the aging process. In Tennyson's very sensitive depiction of the older Ulysses, the poet has the aged warrior speak these words: "How dull it is to pause and make an end, / to rust unburnished, not to shine in use!"[1] Is this not the quiet complaint of many an elder who grieves his or her own diminishment? When beset by the limitations of aging and perhaps loss of independence, we can sometimes yield to discouragement, even to moments of "giving up." Diminishment may take the form of decreasing mobility, painful arthritis, impairment of vision, even the beginnings of memory loss. Do we take this to mean being abandoned by the Lord? Or can we recognize it as an invitation to a new frontier? The as-yet-unexplored frontier of our interior life may still await us. When we begin to turn our attention to the frontier within, a whole new world is born. At last, we may discover a terrain where the wisdom of age is an asset!

Still, it may be harder to talk about living *through* this particular stage because here we do have to live *with* it as well—live with the realities of hearing loss, declining vision, arthritic joints, and many more limitations. A few years ago, these may have been occasional symptoms but now they may be constant companions. (One kindness we can offer our friends and family is not to make these issues the topic of constant conversation!) This very natural physical process might be symbolized by one very painful experience—giving up the car keys. This is a truly poignant moment both for the family member who has to broach the subject as well as for the elder who receives the news. How truly graceful if the older person is the one who brings it up, makes his or her own decision that *this* is the time. For those who have had that experience, you can now look back and see that that was a *through* moment: "It was necessary, I did it, and now it's over." Grieve, yes, but don't feel diminished. Your lifetime value will never be assessed on driving ability—let's hope!

As we grapple with these issues, either in ourselves or others, it does help to know that we are not alone in the experience. The heaviness of loss or diminishment is immensely difficult for the one who endures it but to witness it in a loved one seems even harder. The twentieth-century Welsh poet Dylan Thomas, at his father's deathbed, cried out: "Do not go gentle into that good night. / Old age should burn and rave at close of day; / Rage, rage against the dying of the light!"[2]

Even the saintly Gerard Manley Hopkins cried out powerfully in pain. At a time of deep personal suffering he wrote: "Not, I'll not... / Cry *I can no more*. I can; / Can something...not choose not to be."[3] There's the key—CHOOSE. Choosing to unite our will to the Divine Will makes all the difference. Peace will return. But this takes practice and a strong inner spirit. It's not grim resignation but, rather, loving abandonment that can be transformative. And when at times all our human effort seems fruitless, we have the advice of Jesus: "Learn from me; for I am meek and lowly of heart, and you will find rest for your soul. For my yoke is easy and my burden is light" (Matt 11:29).

JOURNALING

After an opening prayer and some moments of reflection, make a short list of three or four losses that you've experienced. Remember, if you can, the time and place where these occurred. How did each make you feel? Have there been any positive outcomes from that moment of loss? Is there something about it that is still unresolved? Is there something you can do today to turn that loss into a positive?

10

CARING FOR SELF

"When was the last time you saw a doctor, Pete?" Dr. White's face was more serious than usual. "You oughta know, Doc. You're the only one I see." Pete's offhanded answer showed he had no idea what was coming. "Well, a lot has happened in four years. You need to get to the hospital right away."

We've spoken of experiences of loss and diminishment, and at times these areas can seem to dominate our consciousness. But in more "temperate times," when the routines of life are somewhat tranquil, how conscious are we of the need for attention to ourselves, to our personal well-being? Pete's visit to the doctor was a real wake-up call, but the urgency might have been avoided. Without allowing ourselves to become preoccupied with self, we do have an obligation to ourselves and others to exercise reasonable care of our own health. "Oh, I never think about myself!" may seem like a virtuous reply. But it isn't really. We probably don't think very often about the fifth commandment. "Thou shalt not kill" is not a typical point of one's examination of conscience. Inarguably, it's wrong to kill another human being and this is a truth we take for granted. But do we realize that neglect of one's health or imprudence in one's choices that may affect personal health are also included in the meaning of the fifth commandment? So putting off that doctor's visit because "I'm too busy helping others" is not a virtuous act. That occasional shortness of breath that's just due to "rushing around too much" and those spikes in blood pressure that come with pretty bad headaches that are only caused by "a noisy visit from the grandchildren"—these are not wise or virtuous interpretations. Neither is forgetting to take one's medication or to eat well-balanced meals. Taking reasonable care of one's health is a moral responsibility. We are wise to take it seriously, especially as we age.

That's why this topic, too, is a matter of justice to ourselves and others. If we've been blessed with relatively good health and a vigorous lifestyle, we ought to be grateful to God. One big way to express that gratitude is through the exercise of common sense. Perhaps you're motivated by consideration of the virtues rather than by common sense. Then realize that the virtue of prudence (one of the four moral virtues along with justice, fortitude, and temperance) is another name for plain old common sense.

Physical well-being is not the only area requiring our attention as we age. Mental and financial well-being also demand our attention. We preserve mental health by the rejection of the "worry complex." (Sometimes, that's easier said than done!) No matter how tranquil my own life may be, it's natural to be concerned about my family's needs—a son's job loss, a grandchild going off to college, my newly widowed sister. Faith enables us to turn these concerns over to prayer before they become disturbing worries. Pray first of all with gratitude for the relationship we have with these individuals, and then with deep faith that God loves them more than I ever could and that God will give them what they need most. When we are able to turn these matters over to God, we deepen our faith and avoid trying to play God ourselves! We've addressed issues like depression earlier at some length. Suffice it to say here that mental health problems among the elderly, sometimes even forgetfulness and disorientation, can be rooted in an individual's inability to turn away from an extreme preoccupation with worry. As people of faith, we need to hear again God's promise through Jeremiah: "I know the plans I have for you,...plans for your welfare, not your harm" (Jer 29:11).

When it comes to financial concerns, there's hardly an individual who's exempt from worry these days. Many mature adults are already on fixed incomes or are grappling with what choices they need to make before they get to that point. Worry will not change one's financial status one iota. If anything, it will cloud our decision making. Often people now in their sixth or seventh decade have been brought up to believe that finances are a private matter. If a spouse is still living, at least we can share concerns and mutual decision making. But if one is alone and coping with such matters, it's an even more formidable task. Cause for worry, indeed!

Before lapsing into worry, make a list. Investment? Insurance? Revising a will? Or just making a realistic budget for the coming month? Now, next to each "worry issue" put a phone number. Chances are that there's a younger relative trained in the very area of your concern. And as a trained professional, he or she knows how to keep confidences. No relative or former associate to call? Call a friend and ask for the name of the broker or other professional he or she trusts in such matters. If there are no closer resources, there's always the phone book! Seriously, even the government pages list important agencies whose job it is to provide information to seniors.

Admittedly, these suggestions may sound a bit naïve. As a vowed religious for many years, I don't have a lot of experience with managing complicated personal finances. (In fact, the accountants and attorneys in my own family would be alarmed to think that I might be giving advice in this area!) But I do know many persons greatly burdened by such matters. And I know that the business of making a list can be made to work. At the very least, it can stave off worry because it helps us to stay in charge of our own affairs.

Sometimes thinking about others in need eases our personal worries. We can all do something in behalf of someone else. Even if we haven't arrived at the time when living on a fixed income is part of our personal experience, we can and should make our voice heard on issues that are important to the well-being of those in need. Affordable housing, better access to quality produce, health and safety concerns—these are broad public issues, and are often too narrowly focused as if they affect only a few. Our voice may help to shed light on these topics and give encouragement to those working so hard to find solutions. At the same time, it may keep us from becoming too self-absorbed. Having seen in the preceding pages that there is a justice dimension to the right management of our own health and personal concerns, now we are ready to respond to God's call with regard to some of the larger and complex issues of justice in the world.

JOURNALING

Read the Jeremiah passage cited above (Jer 29:11–20). Write down what feelings the passage evokes in you. Then list three concerns that are currently "worries" for you. Can you trust enough to turn these over to the Lord?

II

ACTING JUSTLY

The twelve eager college students sat on the floor talking quietly. They were exhausted and a little overwhelmed by all they had seen today. Dr. Tory smiled at her own memories; hard to believe it was almost ten years since she was in the same situation. This Mississippi clinic didn't even exist back then. Her peer group had come down on spring break to help two local missionaries minister to the flood victims. All they had back then were a few tents provided by the Red Cross. "What brought you back here, Dr. T? It's impossible to make a difference here! We're just a drop in the bucket." Her discouraged companions nodded in agreement. "Well, your being here this week gives me hope so you ARE making a difference," Dr. Tory responded. "When I first came here, I was a college sophomore, just like some of you. At the time I had no idea what I would do with a major in science, but all of a sudden, seeing these people, especially the sick kids, I knew in an instant what I was meant to do. Medical school was a long haul, and after my residency, there were several tempting offers. But the call was too strong. I had to come back. There's still work to do."

Yes, when one sees with the eyes of faith, there will always be work to do. Perhaps one of your daughters or sons or a former student has made a similar choice. It won't always be as heroic as young Dr. Tory's but the needs for our generosity are also out there. We shouldn't think that, just because we're of a certain age, there's nothing we can do. As part of our morning prayer, we just need to ask with sincerity: "Let me see where I'm needed today, Lord." In this age of instant communication, images of world devastation, poverty, hunger, and injustice come into our living rooms every night on the news. In fact, we can almost become jaded by the overwhelming awareness. "What can one senior citizen do in the face of all this?" Or, "I have a sick husband. How can I help anyone else?"

Maybe it's taking the easy way out to simply write a check for the latest "cause." Allowing our hearts to be touched may also be the first step. Thinking deeply, prayerfully, and realistically may lead us to see a possible response. The next step may be speaking with others, even younger family members, who may take inspiration from even a passing remark we make. Is that not one of the ways some of us years ago began to consider the possibility of a vocation to teaching, or social work, or the religious life—because of a family conversation about the importance of making generous choices? And do you imagine that Dr. Tory got through medical school without family support? Don't you think her family back home might be living more comfortably now if she had chosen a more lucrative career path? No hero goes it alone.

We have examined above the importance of the three theological virtues of faith, hope, and charity, and found that they are the virtues or life patterns that bind us to God. In addition, there are four moral virtues, called so because they provide the norms for our behavior toward other human beings. They guide us to recognize others as our brothers and sisters on this planet. These are the virtues ("strengths") of justice, fortitude, temperance, and prudence. Pope Paul VI challenged us: "If you want peace, work for justice."[1] The logic of his words has been proven throughout history. People cannot live in peace when they are victims of injustice, either human or economic. Those who would work for peace are therefore called to be prophets, working simultaneously to eradicate injustice while building the groundwork for peace. "How beautiful on the mountains / are the feet of the messenger who announces peace" (Isa 52:7). This is the prophetic calling for our time.

You see, the call to holiness doesn't end with praying. In fact, prayer may only be the beginning. Prophetic action that is not rooted in prayer may be shallow indeed—perhaps just a knee-jerk reaction, wanting to "make everything right," or a quick, unreflective response to an immediate need without analyzing the real cause of the problem. Real prophetic action is meant to get at the root of the problem. Otherwise, it may be only a Band-Aid response. And the real prophet doesn't choose the role but allows herself or himself to be chosen. Sometimes kicking and screaming, we accept the call. Prophecy for today's world is not so different from what it was three thousand years ago. Remember Samuel? It took at least three calls from God before Samuel even knew who it was who spoke his name! Finally, with prompting from the wise Eli, he was able to say: "Speak, LORD, for your servant is listening" (1 Sam 3:10). Similarly, the prophet Jeremiah heard God say: "Before I formed you in the womb I knew you..../ I appointed you a prophet to the nations." But Jeremiah objected: "I do not know how to speak, for I am only a boy" (*we* might object: "I'm too old"). But the Lord prevailed: "Do not be afraid of them / for I am with you to deliver you" (Jer 1:5, 6, 8). This scriptural passage seems to put us on notice: acting in behalf of justice will be personally costly, but God is with us. Like Jeremiah we may prefer the more hidden spiritual life. Perhaps we've even said to our friends, "I'm not really much of an activist. When it comes to all those public issues, I leave it to the justice people." Well, here's a news flash: We ARE the justice people!

Obviously, the scriptural sense of prophecy does not mean foretelling the future. Rather, the prophet, both then and now, is one called by God to do something very special, often disturbing the status quo. For those who would continue to grow in the life of faith, a reading of some of the prophets can be very helpful. In the liturgical cycle of Sunday readings, we hear excerpts from the Prophetic Books of the Old Testament on certain Sundays of the year. But a more focused private reading can reveal the many levels of "call" that the lives of the prophets involved. (A suggestion: Do the reading sequentially but in small doses. Otherwise, the unfamiliar historical aspects may be overwhelming.)

Such a reading of the prophets will reveal to us the relationship between holiness and prophetic action. Both are a matter of call. Just as holiness is not a state to be achieved, but an invitation to become, so prophetic action is not just a personal desire to do something heroic, but a call to make a difference. Both are intertwined: prophetic action is an element of true holiness, and holiness is a prerequisite for effective prophetic action. (Remember that "holiness" is not "sainthood"!)

The World Synod of Catholic Bishops in 1971 posed a challenge that demands an ongoing response on the part of all Christians: "Action on behalf of justice and participation in the transformation of the world fully appear to us as a constitutive dimension of the preaching of the Gospel."[2] While we cannot lose sight of the larger picture, the person confined by infirmity, advancing age, or economic limitations may well ask: "How am I to respond to such a global challenge?" There is an answer: Think globally, but act locally. That requires us, first of all, to know what some of the issues are, then to study their impact, and finally to make a focused response. No one can respond to everything and no one can know everything, even about a single issue. In addition to that, the word *study* can sound like a bad word! But as we move into a deeper commitment to justice issues, we can't afford to act out of ignorance. Select an area where whatever modest action we take might make a difference. Poverty, for example, is a huge, global problem. But the homeless on the streets of our own towns are a matter we should care about. Our next step needs to be consistent with a Gospel stance, so we ask ourselves: "What would Jesus do?" Well, first of all, he'd probably know where they were and when, and he'd go out and talk to them! Then, he'd confront the local government and let them know their responsibility to do something KIND about the situation. If we're physically able to do these things and we have a few like-minded companions, we could do likewise. But if there are physical or other impediments, we could at least write a letter to the local newspaper to prompt positive action. And then get a few more local citizens to also write. And then write to the town council members who are, after all, our employees since our vote helped to "hire" them. Oh, you didn't vote in the last election? Oh well....

Clearly, homelessness is just one example of a justice issue that needs to be addressed.. Human trafficking is another, and it's a huge, multinational issue. Two million people are trafficked annually, primarily for the sex trade or enforced labor. Twenty percent of these are children. $28 billion a year is made from sexual exploitation.[3] Young women and children are especially vulnerable, brought across state lines and international borders, and literally sold into slavery to sweatshops, restaurants, the sex trade, and domestic services. If there were no market for these "services," the profiteers perpetuating this evil would be out of business.

Homelessness is one thing, but human trafficking seems absolutely remote to our experience or location. We are so wrong to think that. The United States is one of the largest "consumers" of the trafficking trade. No one can ignore this tragedy. Even confined to a nursing home or hospital bed, we can still respond to this evil. Letters—to members of Congress, to state legislators; to be published in newspapers, even church bulletins—are already proving effective, as raising awareness is a first step. One quiet day of prayer and fasting in behalf of the victims of this evil can have immeasurable results. God will not be outdone in generosity.

One final justice issue comes to mind: education. Now that's an issue that's as close to us as our nearest school building. Every politician running for office talks about the need to improve our public school system. And when that person is elected, what difference is ever made? Throwing money at the problem is not the answer. Citizen involvement is at least part of the answer. If you're willing to get involved politically and you're well informed on the issues, offer to run for a seat on the local school board. Can't stand the politics of it all? Volunteer for an afternoon of service at the school every week. If you have a special skill, offer to assist with one of the after-school activities or help the coach of one of the sports. Being in contact with young people in this informal way may make a bigger difference than you think. Yours may be the encouraging remark or the caring smile that turns around a child's school day. I know a genial Christian gentleman, age seventy-eight, who three years ago decided to apply to be a crossing guard at the local school. Now, he's a fixture in the neighborhood, and he knows he's making a difference. Some of the younger children stop to show him their papers at the end of the day. If someone's looking a little glum, he always has a simple joke to tell. And happy mothers even send him cookies from time to time!

It's important to encourage your adult children to become advocates for their own school-aged children—realistic advocates, not just "pushy parents"; but definitely that is their role. If they don't communicate on their children's behalf, who will? As the children grow up, they need to be taught to communicate on their own behalf, courteously but clearly. They should neither accept nor inflict unjust behavior, nor should they be exposed to remarks that diminish self-esteem. Those of us who no longer have children of school age need to attend school board meetings and, when appropriate, speak out. You pay your taxes so you still have a stake in what's happening in the schools. And always vote on the school budget and in school board elections. Don't vote down the budget just because your children are no longer in school. If expenditures seem to be unnecessarily inflated, point that out in a letter to the editor of the local paper, but vote realistically to support what the contemporary school needs to have. As with every other justice issue, we can't stand by and complain. First, we've got to care, then we must be informed, then we pray for guidance, and finally we take action. Do something! Don't be like Cain, who asked God: "Am I my brother's keeper?" (Gen 4:9). Yes, we are!

JOURNALING

First of all, know in advance that whatever issue of justice you get involved with, it will cost you. Select one issue of concern and read or listen to learn all you can about it. Talk to others to identify who may be working locally on this issue. Being part of a team in behalf of justice usually has more impact. Pray seriously for enlightenment as to God's will. Assess your own capacities to be of help. Then act. And always evaluate. Offer prayers of gratitude if lives have been touched.

12

REDISCOVERING PLANET EARTH

"Grandma! Grandma!" Timmy shouted as he ran across the lawn. "Grandma! What are you doing? I came to play with you." "Why, I'm having fun, Timmy. Come join me." Little Timmy reached the bench and climbed up. "Where's the fun?" he asked, seeing Grandma empty-handed. "Why, I'm just getting to know my new friend, Mister Tree." The child was puzzled. "But Grandma, this tree isn't new. It's been right here outside your window for a long time."

Out of the mouths of babes. Timmy was right. The majestic maple had been right outside Grandma's window for as long as she could remember, but somehow this week she was seeing it for the first time! Now that she had retired, she finally had time to pay attention to her surroundings. When was the last time we allowed ourselves to be surprised and delighted by the beauty of the world around us?

The sacred subject of the environment is so vast that many choose not to embrace it. Whether we consider it as the world of nature, a phase of science, the environment, our place on the planet, or the responsibilities of stewardship, it can seem over-whelming—so much so that many well-intentioned people approach it with a "Well, of course" response and move on to something else. It's no different with writers. Acknowledging the impossibility of compressing the subject into a few pages, I could easily choose not to address it. But let me try.

Let's begin with the world of nature. We can start like Grandma above, in our own garden. If we even have a garden, we've made a start. No garden? How about a window box? Not even that? Get a small plant, preferably a flowering one. The point is that nature is alive, more alive than maybe some of us feel on a given day. Watching life and growth unfold can make us come to life in new ways. If we dare to participate in the life of that lovely plant—by watering it, pruning the leaves, turning over the soil—our own circulation improves. Certainly, our spirits rise. But reflecting on the process is essential. It can't be just one more moment of routine. Rather, think: "Something living needs me." Our living earth does indeed need us in whatever way, small or large, we are able to acknowledge. Sometimes that important message is couched in terms too political for the average person to absorb. Instead, tend a garden on a spring day or talk to your houseplant in winter and the connection will be made.

There's a lovely little poem, which you may well remember from childhood. It's entitled "Trees" by Joyce Kilmer. Here's an excerpt:

> I think that I shall never see
> A poem lovely as a tree.
>
> ...
>
> A tree that looks at God all day,
> And lifts her leafy arms to pray;
>
> ...
>
> Poems are made by fools like me,
> But only God can make a tree.[1]

Yes, the complexity and simple beauty of the tree can be the stepping-stone to prayer for us as it was for this poet. So Grandma is a wise woman spending time with her new friend, Mr. Tree. If that's the only lesson she teaches little Timmy, it can change his life. It might change ours as well if we would just meditate a bit. Sometimes we're meant to make progress in the spiritual life just by standing still and deepening our roots, like that simple tree.

But that precious moment of meditation on nature can well escape us if we're too consumed by routines or worry or (saints preserve us!) the soaps. Test this theory out: If you tend one little patch of earth lovingly—your plant, your window box, your herb garden—you'll treat people that way too. Proving that to yourself will take some reflection, and, of course, it's the reflection that makes the difference—that moment of spiritual insight when we let ourselves see the relationships across all our behaviors. What we'll discover is that what we're doing with both the plants and the people around us is nurturing new life.

Do you think that our innate sensitivity to the world of nature might be in our genes? I believe it is. Think of Adam and Eve in the Garden. God's unspoiled plan had human creation surrounded by the lush beauty of his natural creation, which had preexisted humans by eons. By allowing ourselves to rediscover the place of nature in our lives, we may simply be returning to our spiritual roots. Contemporary writers are deepening our understanding of this reality. Father Cletus Wessels, OP, theologian and scientist, affirms the interconnectedness of this new awareness: "The Creator God is found unfolding within the very developmental processes of the planet earth itself and we can find ourselves and God by a return to the earth from which we emerged."[2] He further relates the pursuit of ecological wisdom with the very goals of the Christian community. Describing the Christian Church as a "community of the disciples of Jesus," he offers this challenge:

> The human community must first of all be in tune with the universe and in a special way with the earth as an essential foundation to its call to be disciples of Christ.... [To accomplish this, we first need] to *listen* and to *hear* the Wisdom of God embodied in the earth as well as the Wisdom of God embodied in Christ.[3]

Now, if you're inclined at this point to simply close the book and spend the next year meditating on just these words, your time would be well spent! This is a life-changing awareness, and we can only gradually grow into an understanding of its depth.

Yet still we may ask: "What place does this subject have in a book about Christian spirituality?" I believe we cannot aspire to a complete spirituality without deepening our wisdom about our planet. A better understanding of Planet Earth—its nature and history, its awesome systems, its relationship to the rest of the solar system, and our own place within this mysterious, majestic creation—needs to be part of the wisdom we seek as we strive to deepen our awareness of the all-loving God. In 2001, in an address to a general audience, Pope John Paul II made this passionate appeal: "If one looks at the regions of our planet, one realizes immediately that humanity has disappointed the divine expectation....It is necessary, therefore, to stimulate and sustain the 'ecological conversion' which over these last decades has made humanity more sensitive when facing the catastrophe toward which it was moving."[4] More recently, in *Ecology at the Heart of Faith*, theologian Denis Edwards calls ecological action "radically Christian," reflecting the "faithful praxis of Christian discipleship." Indeed, he writes: "The following of Jesus in the twenty-first century necessarily involves ecological commitment."[5]

To return to very basic insights, let us look once more at the opening story of Grandma's tree and Kilmer's poem. "Only God can make a tree," the poet writes. But God did even better than that. God "gave the tree" the power to make itself! Now there's cause for wonder. Nature has been generating and regenerating itself for billions of years. We can watch farmers plant their crops but the power is in the seeds that came from an earlier growth. We can watch the landscapers plant seedlings that will grow into massive trees, but the power to grow and spread is in the plant itself. Whether we call God Creator or First Cause, we acknowledge his awesome power and give praise. In his prophetic work *The Divine Milieu*, Teilhard de Chardin, SJ, refers to Jesus as "the cosmic Christ," a controversial term in 1927 when the work was published but today much more widely understood.[6]

Nearly fifty years ago, the artist-writer Frederick Franck produced a remarkable work entitled *The Zen of Seeing*. In it he says that the artist "is every man [or woman] before he [or she] is choked by schooling, training, conditioning until the artist within shrivels up and is forgotten."[7] A sad message indeed! But Franck goes on to say: "That core is never killed completely. At times, it responds to Nature, to beauty, to life, suddenly aware again of being in the presence of Mystery." For Franck, meditation on nature "is a way of getting in touch with the visible world around us and, through it, with ourselves." For that reason he advises us to "switch off the world and come back to the earth."[8] John Muir, the botanist and environmentalist who began the National Parks system, put it another way: "Going out [into nature] is really going in [within ourselves]."[9]

Appealing and valuable as this approach may be, there is so much more to our human responsibilities than this. If we accept awareness of our place on the planet as a dimension of our Christian spirituality, we need also to recognize our role in its preservation or devastation, depending on the choices we make. That statement will not be followed here by a list of "dos and don'ts" such as we might take home from a workshop. Suffice it to say that there's more to our stewardship of the environment than the local recycling program.

Dr. Patricia Mische, one of the pioneers of these deeper understandings, reminds us: "What we do to the earth, we do to ourselves."[10] We need to take that one line and use it as our daily mantra. It will alter our behavior, and that of those around us as well. Cletus Wessels offers a challenge even more stark: "Now our childhood as the human race is over and our brief adolescence reaches its crisis point. Will we as humans continue the divine unfolding process or will we abort the process in a fit of helpless self-destruction?"[11]

Our planet is God's gift but it's also our legacy to generations yet to come, a legacy we can provide only with good stewardship. On the most basic level, stewardship of the earth is a matter of moral justice. Justice is defined by *The Catechism of the Catholic Church* as "the constant and firm will to give their due to God and neighbor." Justice toward our neighbor disposes us to harmony "that promotes equity with regard to persons and the common good."[12] In today's broken world, perhaps there is no greater contribution to world harmony and the common good of humanity than our right use and distribution of the land, its waters, and its fruits.

We hold this majestic, productive world in trust for the next generation, and we must acknowledge that today its sustainability is in danger. Our first and most effective responsibility to the next generation is education. How will the young, especially those privileged with great access to an abundance they don't even realize, know about their potential role in the earth's devastation if they are not taught? We know from our own experience that teaching takes place as much in the kitchen as it does in the classroom. It's not enough to go about our business of conserving our use of water (in solidarity with the myriad countries where potable water is not available), choosing to use biodegradable products, bypassing the use of plastic bags, refusing to use pesticides in our garden and preferring to purchase fruits and vegetables without preservative coats (although organically grown will cost more). Let's try beginning a composting pile at the back of the yard where vegetable remnants can be placed, so as to return them to the earth as nourishment for new growth. Any child or young neighbor can readily understand this, and soon other neighbors may choose to do likewise. As we're making these choices, we need to tell our children and grandchildren why we're doing it. We can presume young parents are hearing it from both sides because their children are bringing home the same message from school. Our homespun examples then become on-the-spot education that they'll think about and hopefully imitate once they understand. This is important stuff. They'll get it, but first they need to hear it.

Maybe we're choosing to drive the car less often. Unfortunately, in rural or suburban America buses aren't available as an alternative, so we try to combine trips, not drive off to the store for one item. We may start to carpool with friends and neighbors to handle chores or to transport grandchildren to school and events. Yes, they'll complain because we've spoiled them for too long with each family's private chauffeuring service!

They can get used to it—and learn something in the process. The need to save the family some money because of high gas prices is one obvious lesson. But how do we teach them about cutting down on fossil-fuel usage and dependence on foreign oil reserves? Hopefully, there's a globe in the house where you can take little Timmy and show him where the gas for the car has to come from.

While awareness of our universe, of its origins, and of our global relationships is serious business, we need not allow this new awareness to suppress our human, emotional response to the beauty of the natural world. I believe God wants us to delight in his creation just as he wanted that for Adam and Eve. A daily walk outdoors is good for our physical health. When we allow ourselves to observe and absorb the natural beauty all around us, it will benefit our spirit as well.

From time immemorial, the poets have helped us to express what we're feeling. Who of us has not rejoiced in spotting a rainbow? Nineteenth-century lyric poet William Wordsworth writes: "My heart leaps up when I behold / A Rainbow in the sky. / So was it when my life began. / So is it now I am a Man. / So be it when I shall grow old, / Or let me die!"[13] To the sensitive soul of the poet, when he stops delighting in the sight of a rainbow, he might as well be dead!

Even without a rainbow, the ever-changing sky paints mood and mystery. Each new cloud formation suggests its own depths—sometimes winsome, sometimes worrisome. At times, the forms take on an almost human shape, suggesting some of the personalities that people our lives. Like the varying moods of our own lives, blue skies or gray become a mirror of our own existence.

If we're fortunate enough to visit the ocean shore occasionally, we are treated to another vantage point from which to express our gratitude to the Creator for this singular gift. We delight in watching the powerful waves constantly turning over, seeming to cleanse the whole ocean to its very depths. What power there is in the world of nature! How easy it is to turn to prayer at such a moment, suddenly to recognize the deep oceans

71

of my own heart with its feelings of love and discouragement, hope and fear. Like the ocean depths, our hearts at times are full of new life, at times churning with debris. In this moment of freedom we dare to turn these depths, too, over to our Creator God.

Or we can turn to a winter scene, powerful in its pristine stillness. American poet Robert Frost celebrated his appreciation for this tranquil beauty. In "Stopping by Woods on a Snowy Evening," he realistically expresses the moment when one must pause from reveling in nature and return to the responsibilities of life: "The woods are lovely, dark, and deep. / But I have promises to keep, / And miles to go before I sleep, / And miles to go before I sleep."[14] The unexpressed truth is that he returns a better person for having been there!

These simple reflections, either poetic or personal, are worthy considerations as long as we realize that our interrelationship with our planet must go deeper than surface analogies. The planet, which preceded us by some fifteen billion years, is brimming with life and potency, coexisting with us and supporting us on the earthly journey. It is therefore essential that we deepen our understanding of the living reality of all of creation, our place in it, and our responsibility for its sustainable future.

Will any of this make Timmy—or you and me, for that matter—better Christians? Only if we all internalize the complete lesson and begin to make the right choices as a way of life. That's stewardship, and it matters. Each little inconvenience patiently endured can serve as an act of gratitude to God for the marvelous universe he has created. We say this thank-you because we want this universe to continue!

JOURNALING

Find a favorite nature scene by looking out your window or by focusing on a painting of the great outdoors. Write down what you see. No, what you *really* see. Close your eyes and see it more clearly. Now think about the routine actions of your day. Did any action hurt that scene or diminish the environment in any way? Write down one choice you will make tomorrow that can make up for that.

13

WOMANHOPE

Marguerite was on her way to visit Aunt Mag. She tried to stop in every few weeks. It wasn't hard because Aunt Mag still lived in the old family homestead not far from Marguerite's downtown office. But tonight she had some special news to share. As Mag opened the door, Marguerite thrust her hand out first. The diamond sparkled brightly even in the dimly lit hallway. "Well, saints alive!" Mag exclaimed. "He finally popped the question!" "He did, Aunt Mag. He did! Last Saturday night at dinner! Oh, Aunt Mag, I love him so much, I could just jump for joy!" The older woman just smiled, knowing exactly what she meant.

When was the last time we wanted to jump for joy out of love? Marguerite's visit to Aunt Mag to share good news reminds me of Mary's visit to her cousin Elizabeth. I've always loved the feast of the Visitation, which we celebrate on May 31. You may recall it as the second joyful mystery of the rosary. One of the first narratives of the New Testament, this story speaks to us of the importance of woman-to-woman ministry.

I believe that women have a unique calling to support and sustain one another in whatever way we can, as together we move forward on the journey of life. Whether it's little girls giggling together and keeping secrets, teenagers sharing their dreams, young mothers coping with toddlers or forty-somethings comparing notes on their teenage children, widows trying to adapt to a new life, elderly neighbors visiting a longtime friend in the nursing home, or a wise mother guiding her newly married daughter over a rough patch of married life—women somehow find one another to share strengths and weaknesses, laughter and tears, along life's way. It's what we do—may it continue forever!

The title of this chapter—"Womanhope"—came quite naturally. Women are by necessity people of hope. Think back only to 1900 and the status of women in America at the turn of the twentieth century. Sweatshop workers, nonvoting citizens, mostly perceived as domestic workers either in their own homes or the homes of the more affluent, excluded from most universities and from the mainstream of higher education—this was women's lot. Yet they, like their mothers before them, had immense hope. Intuitively, they knew that goals would become the stepping-stones to realizing their hopes. And so, together, they set their goals. The key word in the foregoing sentence is *together*. Its importance runs through every generation of achievement in women's history. They talked on market day and passed pamphlets among themselves and, without the benefit of e-mails and cell phones, they gathered and met around the country and made their voices heard. The Nineteenth Amendment was passed, and women's suffrage became a reality.

A century before that, women religious were creating their own history all across the country. Many of them were immigrants who came from Europe as missionaries to work with other immigrants from their home countries or with Native Americans whose situations were deplorable. They labored as nurses on the battlefields of the Civil War, helping the wounded on both sides of that bloody conflict. Large numbers of young women joined them, attracted to their life of prayer and generous service. They moved from little mission schools to building academies and colleges, from small local clinics to comprehensive hospitals. The history of the Catholic Church in the United States would never be the same. With no money and few helpers, and often without ecclesiastical blessing, they pushed forward not for themselves but for their people—young girls without education, and the sick who came instinctively to "the Sisters," knowing they would give them help.

Closer to our own time, women who lived through the 1960s experienced both hope and disappointment with all the newness generated by Vatican Council II. Then came the women's movement of the '70s, with all that happened and failed to happen during that decade. Then came the reactionary years—as those in the Church felt that Vatican II reforms had gone too far, and antifeminists, both male and female, longed for the return of a woman's "traditional" role. Meanwhile, our granddaughters and nieces now take for granted changes in the status of women, such as greater opportunities in the workplace, improved (though still not equal) pay scales, and the availability of day care, maternity leave, and the like. It's no wonder our generation is tired!

Womanhope lives on today in the initiative and leadership that caring women bring to bear on situations that demand change. Women are coming together with amazing courage to help decrease the trafficking of women and children, to improve the conditions in women's prisons, to defend women from unjust financial settlements, to raise awareness about women's health issues, to form and publicize groups like Mothers against Drunk Driving (MADD), and to promote new opportunities for the advancement of women in government, in the medical and legal professions, and in corporate boardrooms. Will women be any more effective than men have been once they reach these positions? Who's to say? The real measure will be: Will the world be any better? Meanwhile, how dare we hope to make a difference in these complex issues? We dare because we believe—in God, in ourselves, and in others. Saint Paul tells us: "Hope does not disappoint us because God's love has been poured into our hearts through the Holy Spirit that has been given to us" (Rom 5:5).

While myriad other issues await solutions in our turbulent world, two major issues beg for greater awareness and still greater involvement on the part of women today. The first is the place of women in today's (and tomorrow's) Church. The documents of Vatican Council II were a hopeful starting point. But the hope that the words evoked has yet to be fulfilled. In 1963, the Council Fathers wrote in *The Pastoral Constitution on the Church in the Modern World (Gaudium et Spes):*

With respect to the fundamental rights of the person, every type of discrimination, whether social or cultural, whether based on sex, race, color, social condition, language, or religion, is to be overcome and eradicated as contrary to God's intent....Women's domestic role must be safely preserved, though the legitimate social progress of women should not be underrated on that account....Women are now employed in almost every area of life. It is appropriate that they should be able to assume their full proper role in accordance with their own nature. Everyone should acknowledge and favor the proper and necessary participation of women in cultural life.[1]

Finally, in *The Decree on the Apostolate of the Laity*, the Council stated: "Since in our times women have an ever more active share in the whole life of society, it is very important that they participate more widely also in the various fields of the Church's apostolate."[2]

These statements aroused great hope for the future inclusion of women's gifts and talents in the life and mission of the Church. Yet, five decades later, there is still a long way to go. We can speak with experience only about the Church in the United States, where most would acknowledge that the gap is large between acknowledging the giftedness of women and opening the door to full participation in the life and mission of the local Church. Much ink has been spilled on the subject, and there is no need to add to the anecdotal history to prove any point. It is somewhat amazing that in so many of the contemporary issues mentioned above, women have made such significant contribution of their talents and energies in behalf of the improvement of society, yet we remain underrepresented in the life and leadership of our own parishes. While women represent more than half of active Catholics, their presence as church trustees, finance chairpersons, and coordinators of diocesan offices is scarcely visible. There is nothing in the administrative direction of a diocesan office, for example, that requires priestly ordination, especially as the country is facing a shortage of priests. And despite the fact that an increasing number of women have acquired strong educational credentials in Catholic theology, spirituality, and preaching, opportunities to share these gifts are still rare. Indeed, a feminine perspective on certain scriptural passages, not to mention the value of a feminine style, can offer a welcome change for the whole congregation. In the Pew Forum survey referred to chapter 7 in reference to the declining membership of today's Church, the lack of opportunity to share one's gifts was given frequently as a reason for choosing to abandon Church membership.[3]

We are once more at a new moment. It is incumbent upon women to educate ourselves about current realities, prepare ourselves spiritually every day, and follow the guidance of the Spirit as we continue to make known our willingness and availability for greater responsibilities within our Church. Like Mary, we wait and prepare. Always, we need to examine our motivation. It cannot be about power-sharing but rather about contributing something new and good to the Church that we love. If our energies are limited by ill health or advancing age, we will want to join our sisters through prayerful support. Meanwhile, we may want to look at our own behaviors. If, for example, a priest and a layperson, whether man or woman, are ministers of the Eucharist on a Sunday morning, do I regularly cross over to the priest's line to avoid receiving the Body and Blood of Jesus from a layperson? What statement does that make about my own support of the Church's efforts to adapt?

Another issue of major concern as a matter of global justice is the education of women and girls worldwide. In developed nations, we take this for granted, but in Africa, the Middle East, and island nations, it is not considered a birthright. The United Nations is doing a great deal to assist nations that want to advance but in many places, the need is not culturally understood. Several UN efforts should be noted. The Campaign for Female Education (CAMFED) is dedicated to fighting poverty and AIDS in rural communities within Africa, especially through the education of young girls. The UN Girls' Education Initiative

(UNGEI) is working to improve the quality of girls' education and to ensure that every girl as well as boy receives a quality education. Their special goal is universal primary education for both sexes. The United Nations website has links to many levels of involvement with these and other projects.[4] With the high level of education and leadership skills among American women, there must be some contribution we can make to this globally urgent issue.

In the preceding paragraphs, we have cited many local, national, and international issues in which women are or are hoping to make a difference. What do women have to bring to these situations? We bring heart, compassion, learning, emotional intelligence,[5] a strong sense of "the other" as a person who deserves respect, and a collaborative rather than a competitive spirit. From the perspective of the Christian woman, we need also to bring a sense of evangelization. We care about the needs of others especially because of the Gospel, because we know the example of Jesus Christ. Jesus ministered to others, healing and teaching and preaching in order to bring others to the Father. People today need to know that that is our motivation as well. We care about them because God cares. Therein lies both our motivation and our hope.

At one level, it's impossible to talk about women in the aggregate. The reality is that each woman is so unique that she never "fits the mold." There is no mold. Some of us may suffer by trying too hard to fit into one "movement" or another. We hear apologies such as "I'm not there yet," or "I guess I'm just old fashioned." When reflecting on our own womanhood, we have no need to apologize. Whether considering ourselves from the spiritual or psychological perspective, we are each unique and should rejoice in that reality. Identifying and embracing our uniqueness may be an even bigger challenge. Volumes have been written by and about women, and no attempt will be made here to review their content. Our focus remains: accepting the invitation to the deeper waters of spirituality. But because progress in the spiritual life flows from the realities of who we are, we pause to reflect on the personal strengths—psychological, spiritual, and intellectual—that we have within us in order to move forward.

The advancement of women into all these situations of influence will make the biggest difference if we bring with us a well-developed feminine spirituality. Yes, that means holiness. But who of us is holy? Is that an existential impossibility in today's busy and competitive world? I believe it is not. Nevertheless, just as the aspiring woman needs a mentor in the business or professional world, so do all of us as we try to advance in the spiritual life as well. Call it spiritual direction or just an experienced friend. Either is a valuable discovery early in our spiritual journey. More will be said of spiritual direction later. Suffice it to say here that a wise guide is a singular gift as we pursue the ways of the spiritual life.

On December 8, 1965, at the solemn ceremonies marking the close of Vatican Council II, various cardinals read messages to a variety of groups in the name of the entire Council delegation. One of these messages was addressed to the women of the world. It read in part:

> The hour is coming, in fact has come, when the vocation of woman is being achieved in its fullness, the hour in which woman acquires in the world an influence, an effect and a power never hitherto achieved. That is why, at this moment when the human race is undergoing so deep a transformation, women impregnated with the spirit of the gospel can do much to aid mankind in not falling....You to whom life is entrusted in this grave moment in history, it is for you to save the peace of the world.[6]

Surely, these words are as applicable now, perhaps even more than they were in 1965.

From time immemorial, women have been identified with the role of peacemaker. Somehow, they are intuitively capable of finding the middle ground. Whether it's a squabble between two toddlers or a growing rift between a father and son, the discerning woman seems able to bring them together invisibly. Yet still the world wars on. As I watch the world news night after crisis-filled night and see the pictures of cabinet meetings and UN negotiators, around every table it seems to be only men (with only an occasional exception). I can't help thinking: If we could just take all the women in the world who have lost a son to war and put them around the peace tables, the world would be very different indeed. I think they'd find a different way. The women of Northern Ireland seemed to have done just that.

Finally, when the children are all raised and many of our efforts have succeeded (though some may not), and our energies begin to wane, only our faith and our personhood remain. No need to tally any score. God knows what's been done in his name. In the human order, so often the highest praise comes after we've gone. "She was a true friend." "She was the kindest person I ever knew." "She told me something one day that changed my life." "I never heard her say an uncharitable word." Who wouldn't give anything for an epitaph like that?

JOURNALING

Reflect on just one of these levels of feminine influence from the historical summary, then one from the contemporary agenda. Which one speaks to you as an area in which you have found yourself or which might engage your interest in the immediate future? Then, if you dare, write a one-sentence epitaph about yourself that might be spoken by someone who was the beneficiary of your efforts during your lifetime.

14

MARY OUR MODEL

Aunt Sophie took the bus into Manhattan every Thursday. A native New Yorker, she cherished a few daytime hours to explore her favorite shops and enjoyed people-watching while she ate a quiet lunch before heading home. At this mid-morning hour, there were still a few seats on the bus. As soon as she sat down, out came the rosary beads. "Just enough time to pray two or three decades," she said to herself. Intent on her prayers, she didn't notice the young man who took the seat next to her. When he rose to leave, he leaned down and whispered, "Say one for me, lady."

Every journey is more enjoyable if one has a worthy companion, a trustworthy individual who knows the way and delights in sharing it with us. Renewing our knowledge of and faith in the Blessed Virgin Mary will be a powerful step in our journey in faith. The mother of Jesus certainly knows the way to him. She who walked the Way of Sorrows as Jesus carried his cross will surely accompany us worthily on our journey.

Following our considerations about women with a reflection on Mary seems to flow naturally. Yet some contemporary women might fail to see her as their model on the road to higher achievement, stronger rights, or more assertive behaviors. Women today, especially those whose efforts are driving social change, surely can be said to be "living prophetically," if by *prophetic* we mean challenging society to see the need for change. How can the Blessed Virgin Mary be seen as a prophet? Surely, in her day no woman raised her voice to challenge the prevailing culture. Totally in union with the will of God, Mary was able to see things with the eyes of her Son, Jesus Christ, and she knew. She just knew. Accompanying Jesus on his preaching journeys, although always in the background, Mary got to know the society of her day in a way that no other woman had the chance to do. She was able to see, as Jesus saw, the need for the Jewish leaders to change in order to bring their people back to their heavenly Father's plan for them. Change would begin with the close circle of Jesus' followers, the apostles and disciples, and Mary had a strong but quiet influence over them. She preached without ever proclaiming a word. She preached by the quiet holiness of her life. She became prophetic by her living example. Is this not what so many women all over the world are still doing in this twenty-first century? They are quietly influencing change.

Perhaps we need to review what we know about Mary in order to rediscover her relevance for our time. She is the mother of Jesus Christ, who is God and man. She is revered as Mother of the Church and Mother of All Christians, on whose behalf she intercedes with her Divine Son. One of the best-known prayers among Christians is the *Ave Maria*, that is, the Hail Mary. Just reconnecting with what was possibly our childhood practice of saying the Hail Mary every day will go far toward renewing our relationship with her. All four Gospels of the New Testament are filled with images of Mary, stories of the powerful intercessions she made with Jesus, and evidence of the depth of the mother-son relationship that existed between them. Earlier, we refreshed our awareness about praying the Scriptures, so that now we can return to any Gospel passage pertaining to Mary and use that as a source of abundant meditation. Take, for example, the scene at the Wedding at Cana. The bride and groom were about to be embarrassed because they had run out of wine! They didn't need to ask Mary to approach her Son, Jesus. Just as any mother today at a family party might quietly approach her own son, so Mary whispered to Jesus, "They have no wine" (John 2:3). Was Jesus merely teasing when he replied: "What concern is that to you and me?" (John 2:4). Confident that her Son would help, Mary told the servants: "Do whatever he tells you" (John 2:5). We know the outcome: the water that the waiters brought to Jesus became the choicest of wines and the day was saved! Would any one of us have dared to ask Jesus for a miracle because we as host had run out of wine? Why not? Is our faith so weak that we really don't believe that God cares about our little worldly needs? Mary reminds us that he does care, and that she will intercede for us even in the smallest worries.

But what of our broader needs? Is Mary present even on this part of the journey? After all (or some...) of the one-time goals have been achieved (women's vote, salary equity, work and family, the corner office, opportunities for leadership), compassionate women are discovering that the larger world may not have changed so much. World peace seems like the impossible dream. Violence against women is still all too common. Child abuse and neglect are widespread. Pictures of worldwide hunger still fill the television screen. Clearly, our prophetic agenda needs to be revised. I believe that these global issues constitute the new women's movement. This challenging time draws us once again to Mary, our companion and model on the prophetic journey. If we really dwell on the mystery of Mary's life, we can come closer to realizing what prophetic stance we need to take to change our small piece of the world.

We've already referenced the women of Northern Ireland who bravely came together—Protestant and Catholic alike—against war in their land. They were able to strengthen the fabric of peace, neighborhood by neighborhood. Today, international women's groups are forging native-to-global networks for creating food cooperatives, and clothing "manufacturing" and distribution centers. Local women have opened schools for girls in Muslim countries, where the education of women had been previously forbidden. These are the prophetic actions that are even now providing a leaven for changing the world—at least for someone! A remarkable example is Elyssa Montante, a medical technician from Staten Island, who began with a personal effort to bring needful children to U.S. hospitals for critical medical care—and saw to it that all the essential support services were available to them as well. And this effort grew into the Global Medical Relief Fund for Children![1] Are these not the kind of prophetic actions that Mary would have taken in her own day, woman-to-woman efforts to "do what you can" to make this tiny part of the world a more hopeful place? She will guide us still if we turn to her in prayer as our companion on the prophetic way.

But remember, Mary suffered. One of her titles is "Our Lady of Sorrows." If a son loses his job or a daughter falls ill, does any mother not grieve? So did Mary—when she had no appropriate place for her Son to be born; when he disappeared in the crowd during the family's visit to crowded Jerusalem; when, after Joseph's death, Jesus felt called to a life of itinerant preaching; when crowds of followers surrounded him so that she couldn't even get his attention; when finally he demanded too much of them and the crowd turned against him, mocked him, and arrested him; when she stood beneath the cross and witnessed his ignominious death. This was the litany of sorrows that Mary experienced. Although she didn't understand the Father's plan, she never lost hope. And finally, she experienced her Divine Son's resurrection.

If there is one more thing we modern women can learn from Mary, it is forgiveness. In our most honest moments within ourselves, we are so aware of our own need to grow in this virtue. It is so hard to let go, not only of the hurts we have experienced over a full lifetime, but also of our need even to forgive ourselves.

If our meditation on the life of Mary is to be complete, we see her at last at the foot of the cross, feeling her Son's pain with every blow she heard, with every insult hurled. "A sword shall pierce your own soul too" (Luke 2:35), the aged Simeon had prophesied when she and Joseph brought Jesus to the temple for the first time. Now, at this moment on Calvary, that prophecy was fulfilled. As she stood there, compassionate witness to the world's redemption, Mary heard her Son plead: "Father, forgive them for they do not know what they are doing!" (Luke 23:34). How could he? How could she? Forgive these torturing murderers? Forgive the lying witnesses? Forgive the weak-willed Pilate?

Perhaps the hardest of all, forgive the apostles who slept in the Garden of Olives? Forgive Peter who denied that he even knew Jesus? Forgive all the "devoted" followers who abandoned Jesus in those last hours? How could she? But he had asked...and so she must. And so she did.

Perhaps now, at this moment of more mature faith, with a renewed desire to take the journey inward, we can readily choose Mary as our companion. Talk to her daily. Reflect on her virtues, on her history of miraculous intercession down through the ages. Remember the extraordinary stories of healings at her shrine at Lourdes, of conversion of hearts at Fatima and Medjugorje,[2] and we will not doubt her desire to be with us. If the Holy Spirit is our guide, then surely Mary will be our companion as we persevere in this spiritual journey.

Having refreshed our memory of Marian history and of what may have been our youthful devotion to Mary, perhaps we should clarify some misunderstandings as well. Although we speak of Mary before the throne of God, it's important to understand that she is not ON the throne. We do not worship Mary nor do we adore her. We merely hold her in highest regard, above all saints in her nearness to her Son and because of the power of her intercession with him. Other Christians and non-Christians alike have misconstrued the powerful devotion of Catholics to Mary as a kind of adoration of the Virgin. Not only is this incorrect, but it can also get in the way of our woman-to-woman relationship with Mary in which we share with her our inmost desires and aspirations and ask for her guidance in relating to Jesus. The importance of such an understanding of Mary is beautifully reflected in the Gospel. When Mary learns that she is to be the mother of God and that her dear, elderly cousin Elizabeth is also with child, she hastens to her side. This tender encounter is recorded in the scriptural passage about the Visitation (Luke 1:39–56). Choose this passage also for the day's meditation as you develop your periods of regular prayer time.

In our opening vignette, we met Aunt Sophie saying her rosary on the Manhattan bus. The sight is not as uncommon as we might think. The rosary is a very special devotion, prayed for centuries the world over. It consists of reflecting on events in the lives of Jesus and Mary as recorded in the New Testament, as we simultaneously recite (either aloud or silently) the Hail Mary. Some who grew up with this devotion, often as a family prayer, have set it aside in their adulthood because it seemed too repetitive. But if we understand the origins of the devotion, we realize that the repetition is not without purpose. Although the devotion is often credited to Saint Dominic, its present format really goes back only to the sixteenth century. What Dominic did introduce as a street preacher in the thirteenth century was the effectiveness of preaching on events from Scripture and then inviting his pious listeners to reflect quietly on the meaning of those mysteries as they recited some repetitive prayer in honor of the Virgin Mary and then put their needs and intentions before her. Thus, the Scripture had time to take root in their hearts. From this brief explanation, it becomes clear that the prayer that evolved into the Rosary devotion is so much more than intercessory prayer. Rather, when prayed correctly, it becomes a profoundly contemplative experience.

The more we take the time to get to know Mary once again, the more we will come to recognize that she is indeed a prophetic woman for all time and a powerful advocate for all who journey together in faith.

JOURNALING

Revisit one scriptural scene in the Gospel of Luke that describes a moment in Mary's life. Reflect deeply on the meaning of the scene and the spoken words. Now place yourself within the scene. With which of the characters present do you identify? Why? Imagine yourself now moving away from the scene. How will your life be any different from having been so near to the mother of Jesus?

III
———————

LIVING MORE DEEPLY

Be still and know that I am God. *Psalm 46:10*

15

DELIGHTING IN WONDER

Little JP and his mom were on the merry-go-round. It was JP's third birthday and Mommy and Daddy had taken him to the boardwalk as a special treat. Mommy stood next to him as he sat high on his moving horse. "Yippee," the child shouted as the great machine began to move. "Giddyap!" Wide-eyed, the boy surveyed the world as it began to turn in circles all around him. Suddenly he looked up, his bright blue eyes following the pole that connected his horse to heavy metallic chains that kept everything in place. "Mommy, look!" he shouted over the music. "I wonder how it all works!"

The mind of a young child is filled with wonder. He or she wants to know everything at once, as any young mother who spends half her day answering questions can attest. Regrettably, adults don't seem to wonder nearly enough. I remember as a child wondering why a train engine had both large and small wheels. Good parent that she was, my mother had always encouraged us to ask the questions that were in our mind, and so I asked my uncle, who happened to work for the railroad. By this time, I don't remember the answer exactly but that doesn't matter. What matters is the encouragement I received to keep wondering.

Do you remember the last time you said, "I wonder..."? Hopefully, you said it aloud because it might start a trend. What prompts us to wonder anyway? Wonder is about having questions to ponder. If we have no questions about life around us, about things we see or hear, about politics and war and peace, it could mean that we don't care much. And that may signal depression, giving up on life, not believing that the answers we arrive at will make any difference. And why are we "wondering about wonder" in a book about Christian spirituality?

A developed sense of wonder can be the springboard into a deeper prayer life, even into contemplation. We need to understand that wondering is not wasting time. Above all, teachers need to understand that and to really believe it. In your growing-up years, how often did you hear a classmate being scolded because he or she was looking out the window and not "paying attention"? Maybe he or she was paying attention to something more important—his or her imagination. (Of course, as a teacher myself, I have to inject that gazing out the window for too long might not be in the learner's best interest!) My reference to the school experience goes back to our little friend JP and to all the preschoolers who show such promise in their wonderment. When they enter the more structured environment of the formal classroom with its prescribed curricula, will their sense of wonder be encouraged? Or will it be gradually stamped out by required assignments and "must reads"? If the teacher mentioned above took the trouble to ask her "distracted" student what he was learning from all his "wondering," he might have responded: "I'm learning that wondering is...*wonder-full!*"

Perhaps as parents forty or more years ago, you were not as aware of the importance of such developmental issues, but now, with new understandings all around us, it's important to engage the family's younger parents in conversation about their children's school experience. Often, children come to Grandma's house after school to wait for Mommy or Daddy to get home from work. This is an ideal time to see and hear firsthand the results of the day's school experience. Then, discussing with their parents in broader terms what you may have observed may help to raise their awareness. Parents need to be as vigilant in this matter as they are about their child's progress in reading and math. We all want the best for a child's future, and we want his or her highest potential to be developed, including a sense of wonder. We need to recall that the world's greatest artists, scientists, poets, and problem solvers have all been people of imagination. Today's graduates can complete their studies with heads filled with knowledge, crammed with facts, but they are far from having achieved wisdom. At best, they may be ready to begin the search for wisdom. Their academic pondering of facts may have helped them to arrive at knowledge. But as they move into the future, it's their wonder that will allow them to seek wisdom.

As mature adults, especially because we may have lost some of our own sense of wonder along the way, we may need to work at restoring it. And because many of us are so focused on duty, before we get to quiet, creative wondering, we may need to actually build in a structured time for "pondering." What is the difference between pondering and wondering? I dare to offer a somewhat subjective answer. *To ponder*, according to Webster's Dictionary, comes from the same root as *pound* and means "to weigh," whereas *to wonder* means "to marvel at," or "to feel surprise, admiration, or awe." The act of pondering, therefore, suggests to me a combination of the intellectual and the purposeful, as in pondering the dimensions of a problem to be solved. Wondering, too, involves intellectual capacities but seems to convey also the emotional, the feelings of awe in the contemplation of an object or subject. Pondering is most often practical and finite in its goal. Wonder, on the other hand, conveys the possibility of infinity because its object is open-ended. Ideally, pondering can lead to wonder. It might seem at this point that we have wandered into an abstraction, but maybe that's what's demanded just now.

Today's very down-to-earth world cries out for an infusion of wonder. If our own education and upbringing were short on time for the imagination, we may need to consciously recapture our own sense of wonder. Set aside just five minutes a day for pondering. That requires selecting in advance a subject upon which to ponder, something to be weighed, assessed, solved. Preferably, the subject should not be too personal, but rather something that can be thought about somewhat objectively. Such time is well spent if it gets us in the habit of quietly reflecting even about a practical matter. Then, when we move into a wondering mode about a universal, imaginative, or spiritual category, the state of mental stillness will at least be familiar to us. We can ponder, for example, the causes of a revolution and ponder further the fate of the country where it is taking place. But then we can wonder at the freedom that results, and wonder about the very nature of freedom itself. Looking at such examples, we come to understand how pondering prepares us for wondering and to see how wondering transcends pondering. As we wonder about the nature of freedom, we begin to question our own experience of true freedom. Freedom means choice and then we recognize a new problem (although a happy one), namely, what would I choose if I were truly free, not just from external constraints but within myself? Would I choose, perhaps, to live a deeper prayer life?

"I wonder what heaven will be like": a perfectly valid subject for wonder. With eyes closed, let the imagination explore. See the brightness, all the colors (especially your favorites, because it *is* heaven, after all!). Decide whether your scene is indoors or out, daytime or night, with people or not. Is God visible or just felt? What does the Divine Presence feel like to you? Stay with your imagination as long as you're inclined, without meandering into other scenes. If you're inclined to make a response, do it. Yes, "Wow!" is a very valid response. If prayer follows, let it flow but don't force words. Just be at the scene.

In moving toward wonder, we are beginning to respond to God's call summarized by the Psalmist: "Be still and know that I am God" (Ps 46:10). Because we are human, we need to approach that awesome awareness in a gradual way, discovering in baby steps, as it were, the greatness of God through the beauty all around us. The pace of our busy lives may have forced the leisurely awareness of such beauty to be crowded out of our days. Even though we may no longer be so busy, we may have lost touch with our own sensitivities to that beauty—from the beauty of nature outside our window to the chosen art objects in our homes to the beautiful character of our nearest neighbor. Is there ugliness as well? Of course. But we have a choice as to which we'll emphasize. The healthy soul will choose beauty. In our moments of wondering, consider the source of all this beauty. Yes, the artist provided the painting, the sculptor shaped the statue, but God gave the talent. Praise him and you are at prayer.

It is not selfish of us to deliberately choose to place some small "bits of the beautiful" into our lives each day. Finding a tasteful painting, a well-crafted vase, a colorful bouquet of flowers may enhance our personal space and quietly contribute to our sense of wonder. Similarly, reading a few well-chosen lines of poetry can invite us to a deeper level of truth, even bring us into the presence of God though there is no religious reference in the poem itself. The nineteenth-century poet John Keats wrote:

> A thing of beauty is a joy forever:
> Its loveliness increases; it will never
> Pass into nothingness...
> ...
> [In] spite of despondence, of the inhuman dearth
> Of noble natures, of gloomy days,
> Of all the unhealthy and o'er-darken'd ways
> Made for our searching: yes, in spite of all,
> Some shape of beauty moves away the pall
> From our dark spirits.[1]

Remembering our earlier reflection on the seasons of our lives, we all arrive occasionally at periods of "dark spirits." At such times we take small steps to move ourselves into a better place. Perhaps, reading a few well-chosen lines can restore our spirits.

If we are serious about disposing ourselves to pursue the ways of holiness, I really believe we need first to open ourselves to discover the beautiful in our daily lives. We can widen our well of receptivity to beauty through poetry and the arts. To have no "thing of beauty" in one's life is a deprivation the human spirit cannot endure. Conversely, we can consider ourselves richly blessed if we acknowledge that we are surrounded by the beautiful, if we but let ourselves perceive it. If wonder can be a springboard to contemplation, then we need to immerse ourselves in the "wonder-full." The arts are the product of someone's wonder, and they in turn become a well of wonder for each new generation. If we celebrate each day the beautiful around us, our gratitude will become a prayer.

JOURNALING

Spend fifteen "idle" moments wondering at the beauty you experienced today. Be as specific as possible, noting details of the window scene or the sculpture or the personality you experienced. Then write a brief reaction to it all. Plan where to look for tomorrow's beauty.

16

WISDOM AS GIFT

Lily had been in the nursing home for only a year. She was very much "with it" but felt greatly slowed down of late. So many good memories kept her going. The old friends and family stories were still very real to her. Her aide Maybelle loved to listen to the reminiscences. "I shouldn't talk so much," Lily said one day. "Just the ramblings of a tired old lady." "No, no. Please go on," Maybelle insisted with sincerity. "I love to hear you remember. You're a wise woman. You seem to understand the meaning of your stories. I learn wisdom from you, Lily." "Well, God bless you, dear. You're very kind."

Just as pondering can prepare us for wonder, so wondering can become a prelude to wisdom. A big leap, you say? Maybe not. Whatever one chooses to name it, the journey toward wisdom is the common human quest. If you were to ask a college student why he or she was studying, the young person would probably answer something like "to become a good teacher," "to learn how to run a business," or, even very honestly, "to get a job!" Their agenda is necessarily very pragmatic. That's probably why some of the college philosophy courses are lost on them. Plato and Socrates were in search of what makes "the wise person." Aristotle was said to have carried a lamp through the streets of Athens trying to find a wise man. Socrates said it directly: "Wisdom comes from wonder."

Finding the deeper waters of wisdom is not yet on the radar of the average young person. But with our years of life experience, we may be ready to take a deeper look. From the pinnacle of years, we sometimes struggle to make sense of our lives—past, present, and future. We need to know that we've lived lives that have had meaning. If asked what we wanted in life, even we as mature adults would probably not answer "wisdom." Most of us would give the same answer as that of any young college student. We seek "happiness." The difference is the content of the happiness we seek. The wiser we become, the happier we'll find ourselves to be.

We can make the distinction between knowledge (a wonderful thing in itself) and wisdom, something of a higher order. But what does wisdom really mean? Webster defines *wisdom* as "the quality of being wise; the power of judging rightly, based on... knowledge and experience." In the natural order, wisdom can evolve from knowledge, but it is from knowledge that has been distilled, reflected upon, internalized. Thus, in the purely natural order, the really deep thinker may become wise. The pursuit of wisdom involves a willingness not just to remember past learnings and experiences but to discover the relationship among them and thus to discern the interconnectedness of all things.

The word *wisdom* may seem a bit formidable if by it we understand something highly intellectual. Rather, wisdom can be seen as the distillation of all the truths our finite minds have absorbed over many years of prayer and experience. The word *distillation* is key. That takes time—a lifetime, in fact. Here it is useful to recall the axiom frequently quoted by good cooks and famous chefs, namely, that a meal will only be as good as the quality of ingredients you have at hand in the pantry. Any seasoned homemaker would have to agree. Apply that truism to the matter of wisdom. What we fill our minds with—whether through formal learning or reading or television-viewing—becomes the matter for that "distillation" into wisdom—or into something quite other. Young people who are so exposed to images of violence or even just to lack of substance are bound to be, if not deprived of wisdom in later years, then at least obliged to offset the violence and the trivia by serious, substantive thinking.

Booksellers are aware of today's trend in their readers'

search for books dealing with spirituality and psychology. This search, whether conscious or unconscious, seems to reflect the human thirst for what we have been referring to as "the deeper waters," essentially for a certain wisdom that can be adapted toward life. But is it really more information that we need or is it more quality time for the "distillation process?" Maybe it's time to stop shopping around for the next "best book" and give ourselves some time and space for deeper reflection, time to ask the deeper questions that allow us to tease out the interconnectedness of all things—past, present, and yet to come. We are at that point where we need to journey inward to review the landscape of our lives, that landscape within that has been shaped by all the knowledge, experiences, hopes, and, yes, hurts that have formed us into who we are at this moment. There is nothing in this interior landscape of our thought that was not first part of the external landscape of our sight and study. As the Psalmist says, "I am fearfully and wonderfully made" (Ps 139:14). It is in the distilling of these earlier learnings that we may now know them more deeply through quiet reflection. Wisdom gives us a clearer understanding of what really matters.

At its deepest level, wisdom is not just acquired. It is a spiritual gift, a grace. The great Dominican theologian of the thirteenth century, Saint Thomas Aquinas, in his *Summa Theologiae*, described wisdom as "relished knowledge" implying a "rightness in judging according to divine norms." Thomas also spoke of wonder "as a prelude to wisdom."[1]

In the spiritual order, we recall that wisdom is one of the seven gifts of the Holy Spirit, which we receive at Baptism and in a fuller way at the time of our Confirmation. Like any gift, if the box is left unopened, we'll never experience the gift, or understand the full dimension of the Giver's love for us. This beautiful passage in the Book of Wisdom is especially relevant: "Radiant and unfading is wisdom, / and she is easily discovered by those who love her, / and found by those who seek her.... / One who rises early to seek her will have no difficulty / for she shall be found sitting at the gate.... / One who is vigilant on her account will soon be free from care" (Wis 6:12–16).

The good news is that spiritual gifts never grow old, never deteriorate in power or quality. Now that we're choosing to take this spiritual journey, we need to reexamine the gift of wisdom and rediscover its importance in our spiritual life. And since it is a spiritual gift, the deepest distillation takes place through prayer. Otherwise, it is merely intellectual wisdom such as truth gleaned through more and more education. But some of the saints most renowned for their wisdom were in fact simple, uneducated people. That's the greatest proof that wisdom is God's gift.

Our journey inward, across the interior landscape, becomes the high point of our pilgrimage as we move more deeply into the pursuit of wisdom. There's a beautiful line in T. S. Eliot's *Four Quartets* that expresses this poetically: "We shall not cease from exploration / And the end of all our exploring / Will be to arrive where we started / And know the place [that is, ourselves] for the first time."[2] Such is the seeker after wisdom. The reward is great.

JOURNALING

Reflect quietly on any new insights you may have gleaned about wisdom. Then call to mind someone in your life, past or present, who has been a wisdom figure for you. In your mind's eye see that person's image, hear his or her voice. What word is he or she speaking to you today? Ponder the word deeply. What is your response?

17

WHO—*ME?* CONTEMPLATE?

"What a transformation!" Rita exclaimed as she entered the Sisters' chapel. She had gone to grade school at the academy on these convent grounds many years ago. The little school had long since closed, but Rita remembered it warmly. She had made her First Communion here in this chapel and had her eighth grade graduation in this very place. Wonderful memories flooded her mind as she tried to drink in the modern renovations. The old stained glass windows, lengthened to eighteen feet in height, were now clear glass, opening the room to a world of natural beauty. Light and air flooded the space. Now a retreat center, this was the perfect spot for a day of private prayer. Instantly, Rita knew that her decision to set aside this day had been the Lord's choice and not her own.

Yes, place has its place, and being led to the right place for deeper prayer can be a real grace. Jesus himself went into the desert, up onto the mountain, and across the water to meet his heavenly Father in solitude. The invitation to deeper prayer may flow very naturally from one's regular prayer life, especially if we've become serious about our commitment to periods of daily prayer. Or it may call to us from a renewed commitment to the reading of Scripture. It may be prompted by a single sentence in the midst of a Sunday homily or in response to a particularly moving event or milestone in our lives. Regardless of the source, we begin to

99

experience a yearning for a little more time of nearness to God. Be sure not to miss this moment or postpone it. When the Lord wants our heart, we ought not to keep him waiting!

Throughout our lives as practicing believers, all our activities—daily prayer, pious devotions, liturgical participation—all these moments are preparing us to receive the ultimate gift, which is union with God. Why do so many stop short of realizing this moment? All of our sacramental preparations are just this. The immediate goal is to get the young first communicant or the candidate for Confirmation to understand the sacramental experience he or she is about to have, but the more important goal is to help them to dispose themselves to receive the graces that the sacraments confer. This dimension is not always sufficiently emphasized. So it is with the various stages of prayer. They are good and effective in themselves but they are also preparatory, moving us gradually toward a deeper personal union with God.

We rejoice in the awareness that wonder and wisdom help us discover the deeper meanings of life. But sometimes we become so "stuck" at the level of human understanding that we never let go—and let God—move us into the contemplative moment, into a new readiness for that willing self-donation that is mutual (Divine) Love.

Is it possible that this is God's dream for us? In some respects we've been dreaming all our lives. Once upon a time we dreamt about buying a new house, seeing our children graduate college and walk down the aisle—but we've hardly ever dreamt about our own spiritual future. Why is that? Did you ever stop to think about what might be God's dream for you? In chronicling the progress of women in the workplace, historians frequently refer to "the glass ceiling," that invisible but very real barrier that has kept women from rising to their true heights in corporate or professional life. I believe we have unconsciously set our own "glass ceiling" in our spiritual lives. Sometimes, when we talk to people about perhaps deepening their spiritual life, they'll will say, "Oh, not me! I could never be a saint!" And so we choose to settle for the lesser good, for the adequate formula of living a good life and observing Sunday worship. Or we allow the rhythms of life to distract us from our path. Moments of sadness or loss, moments of great joy and excitement, times of public recognition and adulation—these are all important times that must be lived through and acknowledged. Remembering that all is gift will help to redirect our energies to the Lord. So when a happy event fills your heart with joy, say to yourself: All is gift... and you will know gratitude. When sadness and loss darken your life, say to yourself: All is gift...and you will know peace. When recognition and honors come your way, say to yourself: All is gift...and you will know humility. Then gratitude, humility, and peace will lead you to prayer.

Depending on our family obligations and physical health, a full day of retreat may not be possible very often. But a morning at home or at the parish church just quietly probing the Scripture? This is surely manageable. The point is that little snippets of prayer time may become not quite enough. When we feel the need for more, take that as a sign that the Lord wants that too. Remembering Rita as she enters the lovely chapel, we too enter into our prayer space. Calmly, we compose ourselves, find a comfortable position, begin to breathe a little more slowly, deliberately. Only then can we dispose our hearts and minds to listen. Deeper prayer requires a lot of listening. As we begin, we place ourselves humbly in God's presence, acknowledging that whether we are in a church setting, at home, or on a park bench somewhere, God dwells there also. Ask for the presence of the Holy Spirit to open your heart to his word and guide you to a deeper friendship with him.

At this point, it may be valuable to distinguish once more between natural contemplation and religious contemplation. As we have seen, not all meditation is religious in its goal. The practice of Zen, the calming experiences offered at some spas, the act of listening to rhythmic music as we practice quiet breathing— such activities, while often helpful and even nourishing to the spirit, do not have God as their object. This is equally true at the deeper level of contemplation. Natural contemplation takes the wisdom encountered in pursuit of secular truth to a deeper level. But unless God is the object, it is not a religious act. In his

Commentary on the Metaphysics of Aristotle, Saint Thomas Aquinas points out that, once we have arrived at the Uncaused Cause (God), we have no more need of wonder. We have already encountered the Uncaused Cause, so there is no more need for "study."[1] Now the experience is all about Divine Love. Through the work of our intellect we have met truth; now, the work shifts to the will, which directs our love.

Saint Paul exclaims: "Oh, the depths of the riches of the wisdom and knowledge of God. How inscrutable are his judgments and how unsearchable his ways!" (Rom 11:33). Clearly, Paul refers here to that spiritual wisdom that is the fruit of contemplation. It's one thing to capture this as a familiar Scripture quotation. But when, through perseverance in prayer, we can, like Paul, make it descriptive of our own prayer experience, then it will be, well, wonder-full.

Some of you may be familiar with the spiritual classic entitled *The Cloud of Unknowing*. Written by an unknown spiritual guide (perhaps a monk) in the fourteenth century, it persists today as a source of spiritual wisdom for contemplative souls. I hope you will choose to seek out this thin volume and use it slowly as a guide to spiritual advancement. You will know soon enough if you're not quite ready for such considerations. And if you do choose to move forward with it, it may be advisable to seek out a spiritual guide as you reflect on the implication of the pages for your own interior life. I mention the work at this point because its author offers the same thought quoted above from Aquinas, reminding us in effect that we can't study our way into contemplation because, when we reach that point, it's all about Divine Love. "Thought cannot comprehend God," the author declares. The image he uses is that of the devout person poised above what he calls "the cloud of forgetting" (that is, all the intellectual knowledge, experience, and remembrances of the past), and below "the cloud of unknowing," (that is, the experience of the God who is Love). He urges the pious soul to try to pierce the cloud of unknowing with "darts of love."[2]

Even souls who reach this point in the spiritual journey may well retreat, overwhelmed by the enormity of the moment, as if it's their own work (which, of course, it is not). Or we may let ourselves be pulled back into the maelstrom of "important tasks" (as if any work is more important than encountering the Divine). Grace may triumph at such a moment as we hear the echo of Jesus' words to the disciples: "Could you not keep awake one hour?" (Mark 14:37). Saint John Vianney, a pious priest of the 1700s in a tiny village of France, spent many hours in the confessional as an important part of his pastoral duties. But when Confession was over, he would simply sit in church with his eyes fixed on the tabernacle. One day one of the parishioners asked him: "Father, what do you do when you sit in church all that time?" And he replied with saintly simplicity: "I look at Him and He looks at me."[3] Wordless love.

Our reluctance to abandon ourselves to the God-experience is part of the universal human resistance so well described in Francis Thompson's poem, "The Hound of Heaven." Let me quote it at some length because it speaks to the moment:

> I fled Him, down the nights and down the days;
> I fled Him, down the arches of the years;
> I fled Him, down the labyrinthine ways
>   Of my own mind; and in the mist of tears
> I hid from Him....
>
> ...
>
> From those strong Feet that followed, followed after.
>   But with unhurrying chase
>   And unperturbèd pace,
> Deliberate speed, majestic instancy,
>   They beat—and a Voice beat
>   More instant than the Feet—
> "All things betray thee, who betrayest Me."
>
> ...
>
> "Ah, fondest, blindest, weakest,
> I am He Whom thou seekest!
> Thou dravest [that is, drives] love from thee,
>   who dravest me."[4]

The writings of the saints are filled with similar references. Their efforts to avoid God's relentless pursuit, their preference for the "ordinary life"—such tales are legendary. This, it seems, is the human condition. At such times we must challenge ourselves. Is our busyness a form of flight from the God who pursues us out of love? Perhaps it's time to stop running and turn and face God and just say, as did Samuel, "Here I am, Lord" (1 Sam 3:4). Then the running can stop. And the journey can begin.

But the journey begins in quietude. "Be still and know that I am God" (Ps 46:11).We need to turn off the chatter that so distracts us. Disconnect the cell phone, sign out of Facebook and Twitter and trivial e-mails, and still our hearts. God invites us to go deeper. Here we may take our cue from nature. If we were planting seeds and dug a shallow hole one inch deep, pretty flowers might grow but they wouldn't be very large and they'd only flourish for a very short time. But if we wanted to plant hydrangeas or some other flowers with strong stems and full, abundant blooms, we'd need to dig at least eight or ten inches down. Only then would the earth produce a lasting, fulsome plant. The analogy is obvious. To accept the seed of God's planting, we need to prepare the soil of our souls by going deeper, into the quiet depths, in order to let grace bear fruit.

Of course, one day of prayer does not a contemplative make! But "becoming a contemplative" isn't our goal. Drawing as near to God as he wants us to be—that is our goal. Disposing ourselves to availability—that should be our desire. Therefore, it is hard to be systematic in talking about "ways of prayer" when it comes to contemplation. "The readiness is all," as Hamlet tells us.[5] And how do we "ready ourselves" to hear God's invitation? By quieting ourselves through choosing to live more simply; by maintaining a spiritual focus through praying the Scripture reflectively; by spending our days in generous service through acting kindly to and for others; and by consciously choosing to be alone in the Lord's presence whenever we can.

Many of the saints are known for their "practice of the presence of God." This phrase was formulated by Brother Lawrence of the Resurrection, a French Carmelite, and is well known to those who are serious about growing in the spiritual life. In the early years of the twentieth century, Brother André Bessette, recently canonized, was a well-beloved Holy Cross lay brother who led a life of simple service, and who became known at the shrine of Saint Joseph on Mount Royal in Canada for his extraordinary holiness and for the numerous miracles resulting from his prayers for those in need. His "secret" to a holy life was simply the practice of the presence of God.[6] What does this mean for ordinary Christians like us? The word *practice* implies a regular or habitual action. The "presence of God" means the awareness of God's nearness to us even in the routines of daily life. If we really allow ourselves to believe that our God is so near that his love surrounds us at every moment of our lives, then we will behave differently—more lovingly, more prayerfully, more joyously. Who could not be more loving, prayerful, and joyous if we really believed that God was near?

The life of Saint Catherine of Siena also calls out to all who would pursue the spiritual life.[7] Catherine herself was a simple woman of fourteenth-century Florence, who lived an active life of charity among the poor and imprisoned in the midst of a turbulent society. Committed to the Dominican way of life, she longed to spend more time in prayer. God revealed to her that she could remain in prayer within the cell of self-knowledge even while she labored on behalf of those in need. Contrary to the mores of her day, she—an untutored woman—traveled to Avignon where she urged Pope Gregory XI to return to Rome, "where he belonged," in order to bring an end to what came to be known as the "Babylonian Captivity of the Papacy," which resulted from the excessive influence of the French cardinals.[8] Such prophetic courage flowed from her intense prayer life in which she constantly sought to know God's will for her and for the world. A true mystic, Catherine was declared a Doctor of the Church in 1970.[9]

In our own day, Mother Teresa of Calcutta was another woman, deeply contemplative, who became a major global figure. Committed to serving the poorest of the poor, she rejoiced to pick them up from the gutters of Calcutta, treat their wounds, and take them home for healing care. And, of course, the strongest medicine they received was the love by which they were surrounded, many for the first time in their lives. Mother Teresa's followers now number in the thousands in major cities of the world. Important though their work is, they labor among the poor only six days a week. Their rule of life requires them to spend the seventh day in total prayer. Mother Teresa received the Nobel Peace Prize in 1979, which she humbly accepted, knowing that the example of her work would preach a powerful sermon to the whole world.[10]

Although treatises on prayer and the mystical life can be highly beneficial, the examples of the holy men and women offered in this chapter may be an even more tangible reminder that a life of deeper prayer can be lived in the midst of a busy world. Contemporary theologian David Steindl-Rast, OSB, was asked about the mystical life. He remarked: "The mystic is not a special kind of human being; rather, every human being is a special kind of mystic. At least, that is our calling."[11] So how do we, who try to live the life of faith in our own unique ways, move toward God's intended intimacy in prayer? For that is what is meant by "mysticism." Reflecting on the lives of holy men and women like those cited above certainly helps. They are our models in the Christian life. And trying to surround ourselves with holy people is a wise step. There are among us surely many "hidden souls" who are quietly pursuing God's plan for them as they draw nearer and nearer to him in their daily prayer lives. We have so much to learn from other people of faith. I believe the principle of attraction has much to do with the growth in holiness in all of our church communities. It has certainly contributed to the discovery of the "call" that religious men and women have experienced when they first felt attracted to religious life or the priesthood. Today I believe there are still many generous young people who feel that same attraction. Yet they also feel the pull of the world's needs for their service. These are not contradictory desires. Thomas Merton described this well when he wrote: "We are faced with two critical challenges: to engage the world around us and to embrace the contemplative within."[12] To meet the Lord at the deepest level is not without cost, but God is never outdone in generosity.

JOURNALING

Read prayerfully one of the Scripture passages that depict Jesus at prayer (for example, John 6:15). Sit quietly for ten or fifteen minutes and try to be present with him as he prays to the Father. How does this reflection make you feel? What sacrifice does it require? Write in your journal what you need to do next. What is the next step on the journey to which God may be inviting you?

18

THE PATH AHEAD

It was a beautiful autumn afternoon and, noticing that boredom was beginning to set in with his young grandson Bobby, Wayne decided to be a bit spontaneous. "How about a short hike in the woods, Bobby? Sunset Trail is just a ten-minute ride from here." Bobby jumped at the chance and ran to check his backpack. "Meet ya at the car, Grandpop!" Once on the trail, Wayne reviewed the rules. "Always stay on the trail and stay with your guide. And don't lose sight of your destination. Where's your I.D.?" Bobby reached into one of the hundred pockets of his hiking jacket and produced it on cue. About a mile into the hike, Bobby became tentative. "I don't think this is right, Grandpop. Are you sure we're going the right way?" "Well, let's check it out. Where's the compass you got for your birthday?" Bobby put his backpack on the ground and fished for the compass. Not there. "But I thought Mom...." "Is your Mom taking this hike? What's the rule?" Bobby looked sheepish. "Always pack your own tools." "And if you don't have the right tools, read the surroundings and interpret the signs," Grandpop added. Bobby nodded. Then all at once he shouted: "Look! The sun is just ahead of us! We're heading west! We'll see the sunset after all!"

The rules of the trail are not so different from the rules of life. Moving forward on the road to a deeper spirituality requires a guide, namely the Holy Spirit. We need to believe that the Holy Spirit is leading us on and to continually place ourselves in his presence. Moving forward slowly and reflectively keeps the destination in sight. "In your time, Lord, not mine" is a good affirmation, and saying that sincerely several times a day will help to establish our quiet pace. At this point, several other aids or "tools" may prove helpful. Engaging in spiritual direction, becoming aware of spiritual joy, being attentive to some penitential practice, and finding an intentional community may provide some guideposts along the way.

SPIRITUAL DIRECTION

As we move toward a deeper prayer experience, it may be advisable to look for a spiritual guide, someone more seasoned in things of the Spirit who can "companion" us on the journey. Identifying the right person is very important. It need not be a priest or minister, but neither should we look to a close friend just because he or she is easy to talk to. What is important is that the person has had some training and experience as a spiritual director. The recommendation of someone who has worked with this director can also be very helpful. Finding someone who is geographically close is preferable because meetings should take place with some regularity and without undue inconvenience.

After several meetings of perhaps once a month, the director and directee should assess together whether these conversations show a good fit, that is, whether there seems to be a growing comfort in taking the reflections to a deeper level than merely courteous conversation.

What does one talk about with a spiritual director? Reflecting honestly on one's life experience is essential. The joys and challenges of life, the quality of relationships, encounters in our own ministry if we happen to be engaged in ministry at this time— all are appropriate content for mutual reflection. Always, such reflections should emanate from prayer. Often, the sharing begins with a brief reading from Scripture and a short dialogue about the relevance of that reading to one's recent experiences. Then a seasoned director will prompt conversation with a few focused questions.[1]

It is important for the person who is new to spiritual direction to understand that these are not problem-solving sessions. If a situation is emerging that may require a decision or a response in the immediate future, the most the director is likely to do is help the directee to assess his or her capacities to respond in a certain way and to guide the person in taking the decision to prayer to discern God's will in the situation. One may be considering a new direction in ministry, for example, or a more generous volunteer commitment. In addition to personal energies and talents for the undertaking, one needs to assess one's personal motives, as well as the effect that the new choice will have on others and on existing commitments. Again, the wise director may suggest appropriate Scripture passages for reflection that will help the directee focus these issues more clearly in the context of prayer.

In all of this, what is central is the directee's growth in prayer—the person's experience of God and image of God, and the generosity of his or her response to what God may be asking at this time. As mentioned elsewhere in these pages, the measure of growth in prayer is our daily conversion, our growth toward more perfect charity.

SPIRITUAL JOY

A joyous spirit is both a gift from God and a way of life. It is often the fruit of one's prayer life. How can one be drawing closer to God and not be full of joy? Spiritual joy is much more than just a happy disposition or an outgoing personality. Rather, the joy of the spirit comes from within—serenity that radiates outward, a warming smile that exudes sincerity.

Why should we pray for the gift of joy? Consider your own experience as you've grown in the spiritual life. Was it not the example of another joyous Christian that touched your life, an example that made you see the attractiveness of holiness as a way of life? The bedrock goal of every person is to be happy. So when we meet happy people, we are attracted to them. Consciously or unconsciously, we want to know what makes them that way. When the early disciples were first attracted to Christ, did he not say to them: "Come and see" (John 1:39)? *See how I live...See what's important to me...See me at prayer with the Father...See how much joy that brings....*It wasn't just the preaching of Jesus that drew the apostles to him; it was his demeanor. One could say he brought the demeanor of heaven down to earth. And they saw that it was good.

There is something magnetic about a joyful person. We find ourselves wanting to be that way, too. In her short article "In Praise of Rose-Colored Glasses," Martha Beck has a memorable line: "The repercussions of one person living in stubborn acceptance of gladness are incalculably positive....Become that person and you'll find that, in spite of everything, there is music."[2] But the joy that comes from a deeper living of the spiritual life is much more than "rose-colored glasses." We soon discover that this is not just for ourselves. It becomes a powerful tool for preaching Jesus without even saying a word. And when words come, they are more persuasive, more credible if there is a quiet joy behind them. Our joyful spirit will fill a need in others and attract them not to ourselves but to God, who is the Source of all joy.

Saint Philip Neri, a sixteenth-century priest, was renowned for his joyful spirit. On one occasion he explained to his followers: "Cheerfulness strengthens the heart and makes us persevere in a good life. Therefore, the servant of God ought always to be in good spirits."[3] Easier said than done, you might be thinking! That is sometimes true. At such times it may be helpful simply to count our blessings. That may sound simplistic but it should, in fact, become a part of our daily regimen of prayerful reflection. Soon we will rediscover the fact that a grateful heart is a joyful heart and that joy can then become a way of life. "Rejoice in the Lord, always!" (Phlm 4:4), Saint Paul encourages us. Even when the circumstances around us give little cause for rejoicing, we can find cause to rejoice in the Lord, in his greatness, unfailing goodness, ever-deepening friendship. Cause for rejoicing, indeed.

Perhaps another reservation persists in relation to joy of spirit. "Isn't this just about feeling? And feelings have nothing to do with prayer. Shouldn't prayer be purely spiritual?" On the contrary, joy is one of the fruits of the Holy Spirit. Remember, as we learned in preparation for Confirmation, the fruits of the Holy Spirit are charity, joy, peace, patience, kindness, goodness, generosity, gentleness, faithfulness, modesty, self-control, chastity. Joy is a sign of the Holy Spirit at work in our lives and we should not suppress it. Rather, if we welcome it, it will enhance our prayer life.[4]

Even aside from any spiritual motivation, as people age, many take as their goal—or at least as a hope—that they will "age gracefully," in the purely natural order that expresses the hope that we won't become cranky, grumpy, complaining people. But let's cast that in the supernatural context. To age "gracefully" is to show others that we are "full of grace." Now that phrase has a familiar ring. Was this not the greeting of the angel to Mary at the moment of the Annunciation? "Hail, full of grace..." (Luke 1:28). Well, of course, we're not there yet but, as people of faith, we are "on the way." And a joyful demeanor is a reflection of the life of grace within us.

THE PLACE OF PENITENCE

Penance is not a popular word in contemporary spirituality. Yet it is a topic that cannot be passed over if we are to advance in the spiritual life. If by penance we understand having to do or put up with things that normally would not be of our choosing, then we might realize that we are doing penance all the time! There are many events and tasks in the course of one's day that would not be chosen: but they happen, or have to be done, or need to be endured—and so we do. "That's life," we say. We can begin to understand the value of penance to our spiritual life by reflecting at the end of the day on the moments when we "endured," and then make that a kind of night prayer. "Thanks, Lord, for getting me through that." "Thank you for walking with me today, Lord." "Thanks for being there. You're a good friend!" Whatever words occur to us, this is a simple way of integrating our daily "penance" with our life of prayer. Likewise each morning, as we look ahead to the activities before us, we can offer these in anticipation as a kind of prayer. When we were young, many of us were instructed in offering the works of the day to God as a form of morning prayer. "O God, accept the thoughts, works, joys, and sufferings of the day that lies ahead and bless me with a continuing awareness of your presence in my life." What a blessed way to begin each day! Such an offering makes a prayer of the entire day even if we don't say another prayer all day long.

So far we have been referring to the unchosen moments that we try to face with grace. As we strive to live the day more actively in union with God, we may feel inclined also to choose some small acts of voluntary self-sacrifice to remind ourselves of the sufferings of Christ on our behalf. This practice, too, it seems, may not be as widely engaged in as in years past. Consider first the positive practices—"doing and being" rather than just "not doing." Choosing to attend weekday Mass or church service is a positive choice, one that gives witness to others at the same time that it uplifts our own spirit. Adding a short period at the end of a day to review the Scripture passage we read for our morning prayer period is another example of positive action. Where is the "sacrifice" in these positive choices? We choose to sacrifice our time, to change one of our daily routines in order to draw closer to God.

Of course, we are more familiar with penitence in the way of "giving up something" and this, too, is a worthy practice. Restraining ourselves from overindulgence is a good example. Whether that means choosing not to snack in between meals, not to have that second drink, not to buy unnecessary clothing, or not to watch as much television—all of these can have a positive effect on our spiritual lives if we are motivated by a desire for spiritual growth. We have spoken elsewhere of the need to live more simply in the spirit of the Gospel and in unity with our brothers and sisters throughout the world who have so much less than we. Such choices may be referred to as self-denial or mortification (that is, a "dying to self"). These examples sound like small things but it's the little things that contribute to the bigger picture—disposing ourselves to be available to God's call to holiness.

Some people may be called to live a more stringent peniten- tial life than others. The lives of the saints are filled with such examples of truly chosen souls. Prayer and conversation with a spiritual advisor are essential if one feels thus called. But all of us are invited to "take up your cross and follow me." Whatever we do, whether great or small, as long as we do it in union with the redemptive sufferings of Christ, it, too, becomes a prayer.

INTENTIONAL COMMUNITY

Another support as the spiritual journey deepens might be finding an intentional community. What do we mean by this term? In addition to the many levels of belonging that we refer to as "community," there is that special blessing of a group of other faith-filled people who share our interest—perhaps share the call—to live a deeper spiritual life. What is important to me seems to be their desire as well: to know more about Jesus Christ in order to love him more; to quiet our lives and simplify our lifestyles so as to be more centered in God and in the discovery of God's will; to share prayer and Scripture reflection at a more contemplative pace, perhaps with periods of extended silence; and to celebrate the liturgy at least occasionally with this small group in a more contemplative setting, with the opportunity to share our insights about the meaning of the readings and their application for our world in light of our Christian call to social justice.

But how does one find such a group? First of all, pray to be directed to such a community. If you are fortunate enough to be in a vibrant parish or church community, there may exist a Scripture-based prayer group that meets regularly. The Scripture-based part is important because that should give the right spiritual focus. Also, if you live near a retreat house or the motherhouse of a religious community, you may call and ask to be put on their mailing list to be informed of upcoming prayer days. At such occasions, you may learn of existing spiritual groups that meet more regularly. Or widen your search by going to the Internet and use Google or other search engines to find the locations of nearby religious orders or lay associates' groups. As you search for an intentional community of faith, don't become sidetracked from your daily regimen of personal prayer time. That is what feeds the soul, and the fruits of that prayer is what you will have to contribute to your faith community.

Does this call to a richer spirituality, a deeper faith experience, really happen in an ordinary life? If the call is from God, we will know it. Always, it is according to his plan. Our availability is all we have to offer but that is everything. "If the vision delays, do not despair. It will surely come" (Hab 2:3). We do not speak here of seen visions, of heavenly visitations such as the saints experienced. Rather, we refer to our ever-deepening awareness of God's nearness, of his caring love, and of our heart's fulfillment. We rely on God's word: "Whoever loves me...the Father and I will come to you" (John 14:23).

A deepening desire to spend time with the Lord does not preclude the need to continue the active and often demanding responsibilities of the day. The demands of family, work, deeds of charity, cheerful participation in parish and community life—all these await us still. Pious tales have been told of angels coming to handle such tasks while one of the saints was deep in prayer. I haven't heard that repeated recently, certainly not in my own life experience! So when duties are resumed, how will family or neighbors know we've been at prayer? By the new way in which we perform our responsibilities. Contemplative prayer is meant to be transformative. In fact, personal transformation, that is, conversion, is the proving ground of a life of prayer. That means that a deeper charity, a more sincere kindness, a more luminous tone can be observed by those around us. And in this way we continue the mission of Jesus. As Saint Paul tells us, "It is no longer I who live, but it is Christ who lives within me" (Gal 2:20).

Often enough, the experience of prayer is not all sweetness and light. Coping with distractions is the least of it. They will leave if we don't pursue them. Don't let them capture our minds. They are part of the "cloud of forgetting" that the author of *The*

Cloud of Unknowing speaks about. Discouragement is another matter, and it can be very real. Feelings of unworthiness can be overwhelming, leading to discouragement that may falsely move us to walk away from prayer. The saints often spoke of "the dark night of the soul." Catherine of Siena, John of the Cross, and Mother Teresa all suffered excruciating periods of this sense of loneliness, desolation, and abandonment by God. The mystical poem "Dark Night of the Soul" by Saint John of the Cross has become a spiritual classic.[5]

In his extraordinary work *Four Quartets*, T. S. Eliot offers a line that is starkly apropos to this consideration of the spiritual journey: "We must be still and still moving / Into another intensity / For a further union, a deeper communion."[6] Let us always be open to this possibility.

JOURNALING

Reread more closely two or three of the paragraphs above. Where do you find yourself on "the path ahead?" Write that discovery in your journal and make it a subject of conversation with your spiritual director or another trusted advisor. Return to this sentence weekly to see if there has been any movement in your insights. What next steps, if any, are you moved to take?

EPILOGUE

As we in our mature years find ourselves moving into moments of a deeper prayer life—always at the Lord's gentle invitation—we may come to a better understanding of Saint Augustine's famous exclamation: "Late have I loved Thee, oh Beauty ever ancient, ever new!"[1] But late is better than never, and God welcomes all of us at whatever point, in whatever condition we finally arrive.

If we have read the foregoing pages reflectively and tried to pray the suggested Scripture passages, perhaps we are just now ready to go back and really read the critical pages again. And if we have chosen to keep a journal as suggested, going back to the beginning and pondering our own written reflections may take our experience deeper still. As we conclude, we recall that writing a book about Christian spirituality, or even choosing to read one, can be an intellectual exercise. Accepting God's invitation to live a holier life is a matter of the heart. The road ahead holds all the promise we are willing to discover. Let's listen just once more to the poet's vision:

> We shall not cease from exploration
> And the end of all our exploring
> Will be to arrive where we started
> And know the place for the first time.
> ...
> And all shall be well and
> All manner of thing shall be well
> When the tongues of flame are in-folded
> Into the crowned knot of fire
> And the fire and rose are one.[2]

Thus T. S. Eliot concludes his *Four Quartets*. The poet understands that the power of love is all-consuming. This can be seen as a metaphor for the spiritual life. The passionate image of the enveloping fire in pursuit of the rose of flawless beauty ends in a paradoxical reality: The fire and the rose become one.

ACKNOWLEDGMENTS

A completed volume is like a tapestry, made up of precious threads of influence. Awe and gratitude are the only appropriate response. I am grateful to God for the faith life that is at the core of this work and for the abundant gifts that continue to water the seeds of faith. The Dominican Sisters of Caldwell have encouraged me in the development of those gifts, surrounded me with loving community, and continue to embody the example of joyful women of compassion. The Sisters of Sophia House, in particular, have contributed more than they realize to the completion of this endeavor through their prayerful example and sisterly joy. I have been especially inspired by our senior sisters at St. Catherine of Siena Convent and Healthcare Center, who daily exemplify the striving for deeper spirituality, which is at the heart of this book's message.

I am especially grateful to my family, who have been so generously involved in many of my undertakings and so very encouraging in every way throughout the years. Their interest in the evolution of *November Noon* has been no exception. Friends and former students have inspired many of the subjects included herein. Indeed, they were among the first to make me aware that there was a contemporary audience hoping for a book about these themes.

Especially deserving of my thanks is Rita Finn Menz, whose editorial and technical skills have been invaluable in the completion of this project. Finally, I want to thank the staff at the Caldwell College Jennings Library, whose cheerful competence made every search easy and who always provide an atmosphere that supports hours of quiet discovery.

May everyone who has blessed this humble effort know God's blessing in return.

NOTES

CHAPTER 1

1. *Norton Anthology of English Literature*, 5th ed., ed. M. H. Abrams (New York: W. W. Norton & Co., 1987), 2185.

2. Henry David Thoreau, *Walden*, ed. Jeffrey Cramer (New Haven, CT: Yale University Press, 2004), 325.

CHAPTER 2

1. John Henry Newman, "Lead Kindly Light," http//www.newmanreader.org/works/verses/verse90.html.

CHAPTER 3

1. *Lumen Gentium*, in *The Documents of Vatican II*, ed. Walter Abbott, SJ (New York: America Press, 1966), 66–67.

2. Ibid., 58.

3. Richard McGambly, OCSO, the *Lectio Divina* homepage, http://www.lectio-divina.org.

CHAPTER 4

1. Saint Ignatius Loyola, *The Spiritual Exercises*, trans. Lewis Delmage, SJ (New York: Joseph Wagner, Inc., 1968), 64–66.

CHAPTER 5

1. See James Crenshaw, *The Psalms: An Introduction* (Grand Rapids, MI: Eerdmans Publishing Co., 2001).

2. For further reflection: Psalms 8, 9, 23, 25, 72, 84, 118, 127, 139, 148.

CHAPTER 6

1. *Decree on the Apostolate of the Laity* (*Apostolicam Actuositatem*), in *Documents of Vatican II*, ed. Walter Abbott, SJ (New York: Guild Press, 1966), 500.

2. Ibid., 508.

3. Naomi Quenk, *Essentials of Myers-Briggs Type Indicator Assessment* (New York: Wiley & Sons, Inc., 2000), 1–27.

4. Tertullian, *Apologeticus*, from the Tertullian Project at http://www.tertullian.org/articles/mayor_apologeticum/mayor_apologeticum_07translation.htm.

CHAPTER 7

1. The Pew Forum on Religion and Public Life, http://www.pewforum.org/.

2. *The Catechism of the Catholic Church* (Liguori, MO: Liguori Publications, 1994), 53.

3. Pope Paul VI, qtd. in the *Catechism of the Catholic Church*, n. 975.

CHAPTER 9

1. Alfred Lord Tennyson, "Ulysses," lines 22–23, in *Norton Anthology of English Literature*, 5th ed., ed. M. H. Abrams (W. W. Norton & Co: New York, 1987), 1950.

2. Dylan Thomas, "Do Not Go Gentle into That Good Night," lines 1–3, *Norton*, 2585.

3. Gerard Manley Hopkins, "Carrion Comfort," lines 1–4, *Norton*, 2192.

CHAPTER 11

1. Pope Paul VI, Message for World Day of Peace, January 1, 1972, http://www.vatican.va/holy_father/paul_vi/messages/peace/documents/hf_p-vi_mes_19711208_v-world-day-for-peace_en.html.

2. World Synod of Catholic Bishops, "Justice in the World," 1971 Synod Statement, www.osjspm.org/doc.doc?id=69.

3. National Human Trafficking Resource Center, http://www.acf.hhs.gov/programs/orr/programs/anti-trafficking.

CHAPTER 12

1. Joyce Kilmer, "Trees," st. 1, 3, 6, in *Poems, Essays, and Letters*, vol. 1, ed. Robert Halliday (Garden City, NY: Doubleday, Doran, and Co., 1929), 180.

2. Cletus Wessels, OP, *The Holy Web: The Church and the New Universe Story* (Maryknoll, NY: Orbis Books, 2000), 48.

3. Ibid., 83.

4. Pope John Paul II, "Ecological Conversion," General Audience Address, January 17, 2001, http://conservation.catholic.org/john_paul_ii.htm.

5. Denis Edwards, *Ecology at the Heart of Faith* (Maryknoll, NY: Orbis Books, 2006), 64.

6. Teilhard de Chardin, SJ, *The Divine Milieu* (New York: Harper & Row Publishers, 1960).

7. Frederick Franck, *The Zen of Seeing* (New York: Random House, 1973), x.

8. Ibid.

9. John Muir, *The Wilderness World of John Muir*, ed. William Way Teale (Boston: Houghton Mifflin, 1954), 311.

10. Patricia Mische, quoted in Wessels, 110.

11. Ibid., 223.

12. *The Catechism of the Catholic Church* (Liguori, MO: Liguori Publishers, 1994), §1807, p. 444.

13. William Wordsworth, "My Heart Leaps Up," lines 1–6, in *Norton Anthology of English Literature*, 5th ed., ed. M. H. Abrams (W. W. Norton & Co: New York, 1987), 1426.

14. Robert Frost, "Stopping by Woods on a Snowy Evening," st. 4, lines 13–16, in *Norton Anthology of American Literature*, shorter 6th ed., ed. Nina Baym (New York: W. W. Norton, 1999), 1891.

CHAPTER 13

1. *Pastoral Constitution on the Church in the Modern World* (*Gaudium et Spes*), *The Documents of Vatican II*, ed. Walter Abbott, SJ (New York: America Press, 1966), nos. 29, 52, 60.

2. *Decree on the Apostolate of the Laity, Documents of Vatican II*, 500.

3. Pew Forum on Religion and Public Life, http://www.pewforum.org/.

4. United Nations, http://www.united-nations.org/.

5. Daniel Golman, Roy Boyatzis, and Annie McKee, *Primal Leadership: Realizing the Power of Emotional Intelligence* (Boston: Harvard Business School Press, 2002), 249–56.

6. "Closing Messages of the Council to Women," *Documents of Vatican II*, 733–34.

CHAPTER 14

1. Global Medical Relief Fund for Children, http://www.gmrfchildren.org/index.html/.

2. See Sandra Zimdars-Swartz, *Encountering Mary* (New York: Avon Books, 1991).

CHAPTER 15

1. John Keats, *Endymion*, Book 1, lines 1–3, 8–13, in *Norton Anthology of English Literature*, 1826.

CHAPTER 16

1. Thomas Aquinas, *Summa Theologiae*, ed. Thomas Heath, OP (Cambridge and New York: Cambridge University Press, 1972), 35:117, 161–79.

2. T. S. Eliot, "Little Gidding," lines 239–42, in *Four Quartets* (San Diego and New York: Harcourt, 1971), 59.

CHAPTER 17

1. Thomas Aquinas, *Commentary on the Metaphysics of Aristotle*, vol. 1, trans. John Rowan (Chicago: Regnery, 1961), 66–68.

2. William Johnston, ed., *The Cloud of Unknowing and the Book of Privy Counseling* (New York: Image Books/ Doubleday, 1973), 48–54.

3. Susan Otten, "St. Jean-Baptiste-Marie Vianney," *The Catholic Encyclopedia*, vol. 8 (New York: Robert Appleton Co., 1910); available online at http://www.newadvent.org/cathen/08326c.htm.

4. Francis Thompson, "The Hound of Heaven," lines 1–5, 9–15, 180–82, in *The Complete Poetical Works of Francis Thompson*, ed. H. Wolf (New York: Modern Library, 1913), 88, 93.

5. William Shakespeare, *The Tragedy of Hamlet, Prince of Denmark*, ed. G. L. Kittridge (Waltham: Blaisdell Publishers, 1967), V, ii, 8, 220–23.

6. Brother André Marie, MICM, "Saint André of Mount Royal, Timely Canonization, Call to Conversion," Catholic Online, www.catholic.org/saints/story.php?id=40224.

7. Donald Brophy's recent biography of Saint Catherine provides a reliable introduction to her life and works. Donald Brophy, *Catherine of Siena: A Passionate Life* (New York: Bluebridge, 2010).

8. Monika Hellwig, "Avignon Papacy," in *The Modern Catholic Encyclopedia* (Collegeville, MN: Liturgical Press, 1994), 66.

9. Brophy, *Catherine*, 236.

10. Katherine Spink, *Mother Teresa: A Complete Authorized Biography* (San Francisco: Harper, 1997), 166–70.

11. Brother David Steindl-Rast, OSB, http://www.pbs.org/wnet/religionandethics/episodes/november-19-2010/brother-david-steindl-rast-on-gratitude/7515/.

12. Thomas Merton, *Seeds of Contemplation* (Norfolk, CT: New Directions, 1949), 184.

CHAPTER 18

1. For a fuller discussion of spiritual direction, see Kathleen Fischer, *Feminist Perspectives on Spiritual Direction* (New York/Mahwah, NJ: Paulist Press, 1988).

2. Martha Beck, "In Praise of Rose-Colored Glasses," in *O, The Oprah Magazine* (September 2011), 70.

3. John Delaney, "St. Philip Neri," in *Dictionary of Saints* (Garden City, NY: Doubleday, 1980), 420–21.

4. For a fuller treatment of spiritual joy, see John Catoir, *Joyfully Living the Gospels Day by Day* (New York: Catholic Book Publishing Co., 2001).

5. Saint John of the Cross, *The Dark Night of the Soul*, trans. Gabriela Cunninghame Graham (New York: Barnes & Noble, 2005).

6. T. S. Eliot, "East Coker," lines 204–6, in *Four Quartets* (San Diego and New York: Harcourt, 1971), 32.

EPILOGUE

1. Saint Augustine of Hippo, *Confessions*, ed. Roy DeFerrari, trans. Vernon Bourk (New York: Fathers of the Church, Inc., 1953), 297.

2. T. S. Eliot, "Little Gidding," lines 239–42, 256–59, in *Four Quartets* (San Diego and New York: Harcourt, 1971), 59.

BIBLIOGRAPHY

Abbott, Walter, SJ, ed. *Documents of Vatican II*. New York: Guild Press, 1966.

Abrams, M. H., ed. *Norton Anthology of English Literature (Fifth Edition: The Major Authors)*. New York: W. W. Norton & Co., 1987.

André Marie, MICM. "Saint André of Mount Royal, Timely Canonization, Call to Conversion." *Catholic Online*. http://www.catholic.org/saints/story.php?id+40224.

Aquinas, Thomas. *Commentary on the Metaphysics of Aristotle*. Translated by John Rowan. Vol. 1. Chicago: Regnery, 1961.

————. *Summa Theologiae*. Edited by Thomas Heath, OP. Vol. 35. Cambridge, UK, and New York: Cambridge Press, 1972.

Augustine of Hippo. *Confessions*. Edited by Roy DeFerrari. Translated by Vernon Bourk. New York: Fathers of the Church, Inc., 1953.

Baym, Nina, ed. *Norton Anthology of American Literature (Shorter Edition, Vol. 1)*. New York: W. W. Norton, 1999.

Beck, Martha. "In Praise of Rose-Colored Glasses." *O, The Oprah Magazine*. September 2011.

Brophy, Donald. *Catherine of Siena: A Passionate Life*. New York: BlueBridge, 2010.

Catoir, John. *Joyfully Living the Gospel Day by Day*. New York: Catholic Book Publishing Co., 2001.

Crenshaw, James. *The Psalms: An Introduction*. Grand Rapids, MI: Eerdmans Publishing Co., 2001.

Delaney, John. "St. Philip Neri." *Dictionary of Saints*. Garden City, NY: Doubleday, 1980.

Edwards, Dennis. *Ecology at the Heart of Faith*. Maryknoll, NY: Orbis Books, 2006.

Eliot, T. S., *Four Quartets*. San Diego and New York: Harcourt, 1971.

Fischer, Kathleen. *Feminist Perspectives on Spiritual Direction*. New York/Mahwah, NJ: Paulist Press, 1988.

Franck, Frederick. *The Zen of Seeing*. New York: Random House, 1973.

Golman, Daniel, Roy Boyatzis, and Annie McKee. *Primal Leadership: Realizing the Power of Emotional Intelligence*. Boston: Harvard Business School Press, 2002.

Hellwig, Monica. "Avignon Papacy." *The Modern Catholic Encyclopedia*. Collegeville, MN: Liturgical Press, 1994.

Ignatius Loyola. *The Spiritual Exercises*. Translated by Lewis Delmage, SJ. New York: Joseph Wagner, Inc., 1968.

John of the Cross. *The Dark Night of the Soul*. Translated by Gabriela Cunninghame Graham. New York: Barnes & Noble, 2005.

John Paul II. "The Ecological Conversion." General Audience Address. January17, 2001. http://conservation.catholic.org/john_paul_ii.htm.

Johnston, William, ed. *The Cloud of Unknowing and the Book of Privy Counseling*. New York: Image Books/Doubleday, 1973.

Kilmer, Joyce. *Poems, Essays, and Letters*. Vol. 1. Edited by Robert Halliday. Garden City, NY: Doubleday, Doran & Co. 1929.

McCambly, Richard, OCSO. The *Lectio Divina* Homepage. Accessed August 6, 2012. http/www.lectio-divina.org.

Merton, Thomas. *Seeds of Contemplation*. Norfolk, CT: New Directions, 1949.

Montanti, Elissa. Global Medical Relief Fund. http://www.gmrfchildren.org/about_founder.html.

Muir, John. *The Wilderness World of John Muir*. Edited by William Teale. Boston: Houghton Mifflin, 1954.

National Human Trafficking Resource Center. www.acf.hhs.gov/trafficking/about/nhtrc.pdf.

Newman, John Henry. http//www.newmanreader.org/works/
verses/verse90.html.

Otten, Susan. "St. Jean-Marie-Baptiste Vianney." *The Catholic Encyclopedia*. Vol. 8. New York: Robert Appleton, Co., 1910. http://www.newadvent.org/cathen/08326c.htm.

Paul VI. *Marialis Cultus*. February 2, 1974. http://www.vatican.va/holy_father/paul_vi/apost_exhortations/documents/hf _p-vi_exh_19740202_marialis-cultus_en.html.

————. "If You Want Peace, Work for Justice." Message for the World Day of Peace. January 1, 1972. http://www.vatican.va/holy_father/paul_vi/messages/peace/documents/hf_p -vi_mes_19711208_v-world-day-for-peace_en.html.

Pew Forum on Religion and Public Life. U.S. Religious Landscape Survey. 2008. http//religions.pewforum. org/reports.

Quenk, Naomi L. *Essentials of Myers-Briggs Type Indicator Assessment*. New York: Wiley & Sons, Inc., 2000.

Shakespeare, William. *The Tragedy of Hamlet, Prince of Denmark*. Edited by G. L. Kittridge. Waltham, MA: Blaisdell Publishers, 1967.

Spink, Katherine. *Mother Theresa: A Complete Authorized Biography*. San Francisco: Harper, 1997.

Steindl-Rast, David, OSB. http://www.pbs.org/wnet/religionan dethics/episodes/november-19-2010/brother-david-steindl-rast-on-gratitude/7515/.

Teilhard De Chardin, Pierre, SJ. *The Divine Milieu*. New York: Harper & Row Publishers, 1960.

Tertullian. *Apologeticus*. http://www.tertullian.org/articles/ mayor_apologeticum/mayor_apologeticum_07transla tion.htm.

Thompson, Francis. *The Complete Poetical Works of Francis Thompson*. Edited by H. Wolf. New York: Modern Library, 1913.

Thoreau, Henry David. *Walden*. Edited by Jeffrey Kramer. New Haven, CT: Yale University, 2004.

United Nations. http://www.united-nations.org.

U.S. Catholic Conference, trans. *Catechism of the Catholic Church*. Liguori, MO: Liguori Publications, 1994.

World Synod of Catholic Bishops, 1971. "Justice in the World." http://osjspm.org/document.doc?id=69.

Zimdars-Swartz, Sandra. *Encountering Mary*. New York: Avon Books, 1991.